The Crucial Bridge

The Elijah-Elisha Narrative as
an Interpretive Synthesis of Genesis-Kings
and a Literary Model for the Gospels

Thomas L. Brodie, O.P.

A Michael Glazier Book
THE LITURGICAL PRESS
Collegeville, Minnesota

A Michael Glazier Book published by The Liturgical Press

1   2   3   4   5   6   7

Library of Congress Cataloging-in-Publication Data

Brodie, Thomas L.
    The crucial bridge : the Elijah-Elisha narrative as an interpretive synthesis of Genesis-Kings and a literary model for the Gospels / Thomas L. Brodie.
        p.   cm.
    "A Michael Glazier book."
    Includes bibliographical references and index.
    ISBN 0-8146-5942-X (alk. paper)
    1. Bible.   O.T.   Kings, 1st, XVI, 29-Kings, 2nd, XIII, 25—Criticism, interpretation, etc.   2. Elijah—(Biblical prophet) 3. Elisha—(Biblical prophet)   4. Bible.   O.T.   Kings, 1st, XVI, 29-Kings, 2nd, XIII, 25—Relation to the Heptateuch.   5. Bible. O.T.   Kings, 1st, XVI, 29-Kings, 2nd, XIII, 25—Relation to Samuel. 6. Bible.   O.T.   Kings, 1st, XVI, 29-Kings, 2nd, XIII, 25—Relation to the Gospels.   7. Bible.   O.T.   Heptateuch—Relation to Kings, 1st, XVI, 29-Kings, 2nd, XIII, 25.   8. Bible.   O.T.   Samuel—Relation to Kings, 1st, XVI, 29-Kings, 2nd, XIII, 25.   9. Bible. N.T.   Gospels—Relation to Kings, 1st, XVI, 29-Kings, 2nd, XIII, 25.   I. Title.
    BS1335.2B76   2000
    222'.506—dc21   99-41107
                                                          CIP

CONTENTS

PREFACE

One of the basic problems in biblical research is the very nature of the foundational narratives—the nature of the story of Israel (Genesis-Kings), and the nature of the story of Jesus (the Gospels). To what extent are these accounts history? Or biography? Or revelatory stories? Or some more complex genre? And what if anything is the link between the history-like story of Israel and the biography-like story of Jesus?

The problem emerges acutely in one particular narrative. As the Primary History (Genesis-Kings) is drawing to a close it suddenly blossoms into a form of prophetic biography—into the striking portrayal of two great prophets, Elijah and Elisha (1 Kgs 16:29–2 Kgs 13:25). This prophetic narrative breaks new ground and presents new vivid images, particularly the image of Elijah's fire-borne assumption into heaven and the imparting of his spirit to Elisha. Later, having recounted Elisha's enigmatic death, the Primary History resumes its rough course and the memory of the two prophets is left hovering as it were over the History's conclusion. But despite the power of the Elijah-Elisha narrative, its nature is unclear.

For twenty-five years I worked regularly with this prophetic narrative (1 Kgs 16:29–2 Kgs 13:25), convinced it was important but not knowing why. Though I used it as a basis for a dissertation ("Luke-Acts as a Rewriting of Elijah-Elisha," 1981) and for several articles, its nature remained elusive. Yet its importance was clear. Elijah and Elisha are central to Jewish memory. For instance, to this day during the Passover meal a door is opened to allow Elijah to return—an extraordinarily powerful ritual when one experiences it for the first time. And the importance is confirmed by several other factors. Scholars agree that Elijah sometimes echoes the great Moses. Elijah in turn is echoed in Jesus: Jesus was sometimes seen as Elijah, and in his inaugural speech at Nazareth he explicitly invoked the examples of both Elijah and Elisha (Luke 4:25-27). Raymond E. Brown ("Jesus and Elisha," 1971) has indicated that the primary literary precedents for the Gospels are the prophetic biographies, especially that of Elisha. And in my own work there was repeated detailed evidence that the writers of the Gospels, especially the author of Luke-Acts, made deliberate literary use of the Elijah-Elisha narrative.

However, it was only in 1995, while working on Genesis and the overall unity of the Primary History, that the basic reason for the importance of Elijah and Elisha finally began to emerge: the Elijah-Elisha narrative is so written that it distills the entire Primary History. It is not just Moses who is echoed in this narrative; so are Genesis, Joshua, Judges, 1 and 2 Samuel, and the rest of 1 and 2 Kings. While the beginning of Genesis, for instance, is dominated by the unforgettable story of a great flood, Elijah's history, with a kind of inverse artistry, begins with a great drought. Like a deep-seeing mirror near the end of a long busy room, the Elijah-Elisha narrative absorbs the whole scene of the Primary History and reflects it in a way that shows its essence. It synthesizes and interprets. Thus the nature of the Elijah-Elisha narrative begins to emerge: to a significant degree it is an interpretive synthesis of a larger narrative.

Basic to this interpretation is a shift of emphasis from history to biography and from history to prophecy. The deep-seeing mirror gives priority not to patriarchs or kings but to prophets and the prophetic word—ultimately the word of God.

This priority of prophecy applies also to Elijah and Elisha themselves: whatever their actual history, the present narrative reshapes the details of that history for a larger purpose—to portray them precisely as prophets and as quintessential bearers of God's word. Their biographies are not so much personal accounts as distillations of God's word in history. These biographies capture the essence both of history and of God.

The Elijah-Elisha narrative, however, is not only a distillation of the Primary History. It is also a literary model for the Gospels.

The Gospels of course are quite different—distinct in content and in complexity of genre. But the Gospels' foundational model is the Elijah-Elisha narrative. By shifting the emphasis of the Primary History—from history toward biography, and from history toward the (prophetic) word—the account of Elijah and Elisha prepared the literary way for the writing of the Gospels. Thus the Elijah-Elisha narrative constitutes the key bridge between the foundational narratives of Judaism and Christianity.

These two ideas—the Elijah-Elisha narrative synthesizes the Primary History and provides a basic model for the gospels—are relatively simple, but their details are immensely complex, and it is not possible for the present writer to embark on a full analysis. What is given here is a summary demonstration; brief, but hopefully sufficient to communicate the essential thesis and to prepare the ground for further research. Such research should contribute in turn to a clearer sense of the very nature of biblical narrative.

In this brief study, priority goes to the first part of the thesis—to the role of the Elijah-Elisha narrative as an interpretive synthesis of the Primary History. The second part—Elijah-Elisha as a model for the Gospels—has already been begun by others and must await a much longer study.

INTRODUCTION

Since the 1970s there has been increasing evidence that texts which at first sight appear fragmented are in fact unified. This applies to both the Pentateuch and the Deuteronomic History.[1] For instance, where Martin Noth once maintained that Numbers is deeply fragmented (1968),[2] Mary Douglas has given strong evidence of its unity (1993).[3] Evidence is also beginning to emerge for the unity of the Primary History as a whole.[4]

A particularly striking example of the emergence of unity occurs in the case of Judges. This book, with its succession of diverse

---

[1] See, for example, Jan Fokkelman, *Narrative Art in Genesis: Specimens of Stylistic and Structural Analysis,* Studia Semitica Neerlandica 17 (Assen: Van Gorcum, 1975); Robert Alter, *The Art of Biblical Narrative* (New York: Basic Books, 1981); Robert Polzin, *Moses and the Deuteronomist: A Literary Study of the Deuteronomic History,* part 1 (Bloomington and Indianapolis: Indiana University Press, 1980); V. Philips Long, *The Reign and Rejection of King Saul: A Case for Literary and Theological Coherence,* SBLDS 118 (Atlanta: Scholars Press, 1989); David M. Gunn, ed., *Narrative and Novella in Samuel: Studies by Hugo Gressmann and Other Scholars 1906–1923,* JSOTSS 116 (Sheffield: Almond Press, 1991); Herbert Chanan Brichto, *The Names of God* (New York/Oxford: Oxford University Press, 1998).

[2] Martin Noth, *Numbers: A Commentary* (London: SCM Press, 1968).

[3] Mary Douglas, *In the Wilderness: The Doctrine of Defilement in the Book of Numbers,* JSOTSS 158 (Sheffield: JSOT Press, 1993).

[4] David Noel Freedman, *The Unity of the Hebrew Bible* (Ann Arbor: University of Michigan Press, 1991).

characters, some major, others miniscule, was often regarded as a form of crude necklace—a collection of rugged traditions which were essentially independent of one another and which served primarily as reflections of diverse historical events. Now, however, the emphasis has changed: the work of several researchers, especially Cheryl Exum, Ji-chan Kim, and Barry Webb,[5] shows that the apparently disparate stories are pervasively interconnected. At times this unity has an "architectonic tightness."[6]

Nobody has yet done for the Elijah-Elisha narrative what authors such as Exum, Kim, and Webb have done for the book of Judges—rescue it from alleged fragmentation and show the coherence of the present text. As with earlier research on Judges, the quest for history—for underlying traditions—has tended to obscure the existing account. In particular, the Elijah-Elisha narrative has often been read as consisting largely of two independent units, two cycles of tradition.[7]

---

[5] Cheryl J. Exum, "Literary Patterns in the Samson Saga: An Investigation of Rhetorical Style in Biblical Prose" (Ph.D. diss., Columbia University, New York, 1976); Cheryl J. Exum, "Promise and Fulfilment: Narrative Art in Judges 13," *JBL* 99 (1980) 43–59; Cheryl J. Exum, "Aspects of Symmetry and Balance in the Samson Saga," *JSOT* 19 (1981) 3–29; Ji-chan Kim, *The Structure of the Samson Cycle* (Kampen: Pharos, 1993); Barry G. Webb, *The Book of Judges: An Integrated Reading,* JSOTSS 46 (Sheffield: JSOT Press, 1987).

[6] Kim, *The Samson Cycle,* 424.

[7] On Elijah and Elisha, see J. Maxwell Miller, "The Elisha Cycle and the Accounts of the Omride Wars," *JBL* 85 (1966) 441–54; Leah Bronner, *The Stories of Elijah and Elisha as Polemics against Baal Worship* (Leiden: Brill, 1968); Georg Fohrer, *Elia,* 2d ed., AThANT 53 (Zürich: Zwingli, 1968); and especially Hans-Christoph Schmitt, *Elisa. Traditionsgeschichtliche Untersuchungen* (Gütersloh: Gerd Mohn, 1972); Burke Long, "2 Kings III and Genres of Prophetic Narrative," *VT* 23 (1973) 337–48; Harald Schweizer, *Elischa in den Kriegen. Literaturwissenschaftliche Untersuchung von 1 Kön 3; 6,8-23; 6:24–7:20,* SANT 37 (München: Kösel, 1974); Rudolph Smend, "Der Biblische und der Historische Elia," *Congress Volume. Edinburgh 1974,* 167–184, VTS 28 (Leiden: Brill, 1975); and Jerome T. Walsh, "The Elijah Cycle: A Synchronic Approach" (Ph.D. diss., University of Michigan, 1982). Even the recent work of

The Elijah-Elisha narrative is indeed twofold—it clearly highlights two main prophets—but it is also a careful unity, as closely knit as Judges.

The purpose of this study is, first, to give indications of that unity (Chapter 1), next, to show briefly that the Elijah-Elisha narrative is an interpretive synthesis of the Primary History (Chapters 2–4), and, finally, to strengthen the claim that the Elijah-Elisha narrative was a literary model for the Gospels (Chapter 5).

Hermann-Josef Stipp on Elisha (*Elischa-Propheten-Gottesmänner,* Münchener Universitätsschriften [St. Ottilien: EOS, 1987]), despite its original contribution, effectively isolates 1 Kgs 20:22 and 2 Kings 2–7 from the larger context (1 Kings 17–2 Kings 13). Winfried Thiel ("Deuteronomistische Redaktionsarbeit in den Elia-Erzählungen," *Congress Volume. Leuven 1989,* ed. J. A. Emerton, 148–71, VTS 43 [Leiden: Brill, 1991]) develops the idea of the relationship of some Elijah stories (1 Kings 17–19) to the larger deuteronomic history, yet he does not pursue the possibility of a close relationship to the larger Elijah-Elisha narrative. Jerome Walsh (*1 Kings,* Berit Olam [Collegeville: The Liturgical Press, 1996]) offers a fresh approach, but his assignment does not include Elisha. Alexander Rofé (*The Prophetical Stories: The Narratives about the Prophets in the Hebrew Bible: Their Literary Types and History* [Jerusalem: Magnes, 1988]) and Miguel Alvarez Barredo (*Las narraciones sobre Elías y Eliseo en los libros de los Reyes: Formación y teología,* Publicaciones Instituto Teológico Franciscano Serie Mayor 21 [Murcia, Spain: Espigas, 1997]), while insightful, spend insufficient time with the finished text before discussing conjectural earlier stages. As Richard Sarason ("Towards a New Agendum for the Study of Rabbinic Midrashic Literature," *Studies in Aggadah, Targum and Jewish Liturgy in Memory of Joseph Heinemann,* ed. E. Fleischer and J. J. Peuchowski, 61 [Jerusalem: Magnes, 1981]) would say, they pose the historical question prematurely. Phyllis Trible ("Exegesis for Storytellers and Other Strangers," *JBL* 114 [1995] 3–19) shows some of the continuities within the text. On Elijah in Jewish memory, see Aharon Wiener, *The Prophet Elijah in the Development of Judaism: A Depth Psychological Study,* Littman Library of Jewish Civilization (London/Henley/Boston: Routledge & Kegan Paul, 1978).

The lack of progress in dealing with the Elijah-Elisha narrative as a whole is illustrated in Iain Provan's review of research on 1 and 2 Kings (*1 & 2 Kings,* Old Testament Guides [Sheffield: Sheffield Academic, 1997]): essentially there is nothing to report.

Even if one disagrees with the thesis concerning the narrative's unity—or at least with the details of that thesis—it is still possible to ask whether the narrative reflects the Primary History in some way. The well-established claim that Elijah reflects Moses was not dependent on any theory of narrative unity; and neither is the larger claim about reflecting the entire Primary History. The thesis of unity therefore is not indispensable. But it helps.

ABBREVIATIONS

AB	Anchor Bible
AThANT	Abhandlungen zur Theologie des Alten und Neuen Testaments
BETL	Bibliotheca ephemeridum theologicarum Lovaniensium
Bib	*Biblica*
BIS	Biblical Interpretation Series
CBQ	*Catholic Biblical Quarterly*
ExpTim	*Expository Times*
JBC	*The Jerome Biblical Commentary*
JBL	*Journal of Biblical Literature*
JR	*Journal of Religion*
JSOT	*Journal for the Study of the Old Testament*
JSOTSS	Journal for the Study of the Old Testament Supplement Series
NTS	Novum Testamentum, Supplements
NTAbh	Neutestamentliche Abhandlungen
RHPR	*Revue d'histoire et de philosophie religieuses*
SANT	Studien zum Alten und Neuen Testament
SBLDS	SBL Dissertation Series
SNTA	Studiorum Novi Testamenti Auxilia
SNTSMS	Society for New Testament Studies Monograph Series
ST	*Studia Theologica*
VT	*Vetus Testamentum*
VTS	Vetus Testamentum Supplements

CHAPTER 1

THE UNITY OF
THE ELIJAH-ELISHA NARRATIVE

The Elijah-Elisha narrative consists of 1 Kgs 16:29–2 Kgs 13:25 (nineteen chapters and one paragraph). Several studies, including the present writer's dissertation,[1] have sometimes made the mistake of limiting the narrative to fourteen chapters (1 Kings 17–2 Kings 8) or less. But the text goes further—in both directions.

The narrative begins not with the appearance of Elijah (1 Kings 17) but with the preceding description of a great crisis—the introduction to the evil of Ahab and Jezebel (1 Kgs 16:29-34). This portrait of Ahab and Jezebel, with its concluding reference to how Hiel of Bethel rebuilt Jericho at the cost of his own two sons (1 Kgs 16:34), sets the scene for what follows.[2] The basic content of this scene-setting picture is stark: idolatry and death. The idolatry

---

[1] Thomas L. Brodie, "Luke the Literary Interpreter: Luke-Acts as a Systematic Rewriting and Updating of the Elijah-Elisha Narrative" (Ph.D. diss., University of St. Thomas, 1981). As well as being incomplete, section 6A of the dissertation is substantially wrong (pp. 289–301). Otherwise the general thesis is valid.

[2] Charles Conroy, "Hiel between Ahab and Elijah-Elisha: 1 Kings 16,34 in Its Immediate Literary Context," *Bib* 77 (1996) 210–8; see Alan J. Hauser and Russel Gregory, *From Carmel to Horeb: Elijah in Crisis,* Bible and Literature 19 (Sheffield: Almond, 1990) 12; Phyllis Trible, "Exegesis for Storytellers and Other Strangers," *JBL* 114 (1995) 3–4.

of Ahab and Jezebel provides a foil for the prophets' clear sense of the true God. And Hiel's murder of his own two sons constitutes a brutal contrast with the prophets' struggle to preserve life, especially the lives of endangered children (the children of the widows, 1 Kgs 17:7-24; 2 Kgs 4:1-7; and the child of the Shunammitess 2 Kgs 4:8-37).

The narrative ends not with the conclusion of Elisha's active ministry, his appearance in Damascus (2 Kings 8), but with the events that flow from his prophetic word, events which include Jehu's coup and the coup's repercussions in Jerusalem (2 Kings 9–12). The inclusion of the Jehu-Jerusalem sequence is confirmed by its position in the text—*before* the wondrous death of Elisha (2 Kings 13).

INDICATIONS OF UNITY

There are at least four indications that the Elijah-Elisha account is a unity: (1) it constitutes a succession narrative, (2) it is bound together by prophecy, (3) it has a unique emphasis on healing, (4) it has a coherent structure.

Ideally the discussion of structure should come first. In the words of R. I. Letellier:

> The first concern in analyzing any biblical text is to ascertain its limits, where it begins as a literary unit and where it ends. J. Muilenberg [1969, 9] has established this as a first principle of rhetorical criticism. . . . He asserts that the literary unit is "an indissoluble whole, an artistic and creative unity the contours of which must be perceived if the central preoccupation or dominant motif invariably stated at the beginning is to be resolved."[3]

Structure, therefore, is foundational; it clarifies where the various units begin and end. However, in order to establish a general acquaintance with the narrative as a whole it seems appropriate to commence with general features: succession, prophecy, and healing.

---

[3] Robert I. Letellier, *Day in Mamre Night in Sodom: Abraham and Lot in Genesis 18 and 19,* BIS 10 (Leiden/New York/Köln: Brill, 1995) 30.

INITIAL INDICATIONS:
SUCCESSION, PROPHECY, HEALING

THE UNITY OF A SUCCESSION NARRATIVE

The stories surrounding the two great prophets are not two disparate collections. A discussion in South Africa about the nature of the Elijah-Elisha narrative quickly revealed one of its basic unifying features: it constitutes a succession narrative, a variation on the succession narrative of David and Solomon.[4] This does not mean tying the Elijah-Elisha narrative to one of the many hypotheses about the David-Solomon story,[5] but simply that the general picture of a succession, especially as seen in the David-Solomon story, provides an initial approach to the unity of the Elijah-Elisha narrative.

The idea that the Elijah-Elisha narrative constitutes some kind of succession narrative is not altogether new. As was remarked decades ago, Elijah and Elisha "provide the only example in the Old Testament of a prophet appointing his own prophetic successor";[6] in fact, these two prophets exemplify the basic idea of prophetic succession.[7] The reality of this succession is seen in the detailed continuity—ideological and literary—between the two parts of the narrative.[8]

Some of that continuity may be noted: the prophets' names, their vocations, the calling of one by the other, the passing of the mantle as to a first-born son (1 Kgs 19:19-21; 2 Kgs 2:7-14), and Elisha's fulfilling of Elijah's mission (to anoint Hazael and Jehu, 1 Kgs 19:15-16; 2 Kgs 8:7-15; 9:1-3).

---

[4] Ed Doherty, S.J., in conversation, June 6, 1994, St. Joseph's Scholasticate, Cedara, KwaZulu-Natal.

[5] For a review of hypotheses, see Gillian Keys, *The Wages of Sin: A Reappraisal of the "Succession Narrative,"* JSOTSS 221 (Sheffield: Academic Press, 1996) 14–42.

[6] Robert P. Carroll, "The Elijah-Elisha Sagas: Some Remarks on Prophetic Succession in Ancient Israel," *VT* 19 (1969) 403.

[7] Ibid., 408.

[8] R. A. Carlson, "Élisée: Le successeur d'Élie," *VT* 20 (1970) 385–405.

There is continuity also in specific people and actions. For instance, the figure of the woman in 1 Kings 17 occurs in more intensified form in the women of 2 Kings 4. The Aramean wars, already serious in 1 Kings 20 and 22, become worse in 2 Kings 6–8. Both war accounts (in 1 and 2 Kings) tell, for example, in varying ways, of how Ben-haded, having besieged Samaria with terrible intensity, was routed, suddenly and totally (1 Kgs 20:1-21; 2 Kgs 6:24–7:20). There is complementarity also between the two accounts of how Syrian attackers were overcome and were then received with gestures of friendship (1 Kgs 20:22-43; 2 Kgs 6:8-23).

These brief observations do not do justice to the full range of continuities between Elijah and Elisha, but they reinforce the impression that the Elijah-Elisha text is indeed some form of succession narrative and, as such, some form of unity.

THE UNITY OF PROPHECY

The identity of the narrative comes from its two central characters: Elijah, who appears suddenly in 1 Kings 17, and Elisha, who dies in 2 Kings 13. Set amid the flow of kings, the account of the two prophets entails a switch of emphasis from history to a form of biography.

Yet the defining feature of this narrative is not history or biography. It is prophecy, or, more precisely, the prophetic word, the divine word that pervades not only the lives of Elijah and Elisha but also the lives of various other prophets who are mentioned. Apart from some formulaic passages (the repetitive summaries of dates and reigns: 1 Kgs 22:39-54; 2 Kgs 3:1-3; 8:16-29; 10:28-36; 13:1-13), passages that link the Elijah-Elisha story with the rest of 1 and 2 Kings, every single episode in the entire narrative is governed by prophecy or follows from prophecy.[9] This includes not only the massacres of Jehu, the prophetically-appointed king (1 Kgs 19:16-17; 2 Kgs 9:1-3), but also the subsequent story of Athaliah and Joash in the Jerusalem Temple (2 Kings 11–12; cf. 9:27; 11:1). The Temple story (Athaliah-Joash), even though it does not mention a prophet, receives its momentum from the Jehu

---

[9] See ibid., 401.

story. For instance, the killing of Athaliah (2 Kgs 11:13-16) has echoes of Jehu's prophecy-fulfilling killing of Jezebel (2 Kgs 9:30-39). And Joash's repairing of the Temple (2 Kings 12) is set against the foil of Jehu's demolition of the temple of Baal (2 Kgs 10:18-27). The entire narrative, then, from the opening declaration of Elijah (1 Kgs 17:1) to the final episodes concerning the Temple and the death of Elisha (2 Kings 11–13), is woven in a web of prophecy.

Therefore, the multiplicity of prophets—prophets other than Elijah and Elisha—indicates not that the narrative is loose or confused, but that its defining focus is on something more basic than biography: the divine word.

The word takes diverse forms, but among these forms there is continuity. At first, during the great drought (1 Kgs 16:29–18:46, esp. ch. 17) the word is like the word of creation, ruling both nature and humanity in a pattern of command-and-compliance.[10] In the final stages, when much of the action occurs in Jerusalem (2 Kings 11–13, esp. ch. 11), the pattern is still one of command-and-compliance, but in a down-to-earth way: the word of command-and-compliance, issuing from the chief priest and communicated through the ranks of the army, effectively saves Jerusalem and the Temple (2 Kings 11, esp. 11:4-16). Thus the power of the divine word, as illustrated in the pattern of command-and-compliance, forms an *inclusio* which encompasses the prophetic narrative, from the creation-related commands at the beginning (1 Kings 17) to the down-to-earth temple-related military commands near the end (2 Kings 11). Elisha's dying words continue the pattern of command-and-compliance (13:14-19).

Overall, then, the power of the (prophetic) word is a further factor binding the Elijah-Elisha narrative into a unity.

Unique Emphasis on Healing

The Elijah-Elisha narrative contains a unique emphasis on miracles, extraordinary deeds performed by humans rather than

---

[10] Jerome T. Walsh, *1 Kings,* Berit Olam (Collegeville: The Liturgical Press, 1996) 228.

by God. In fact, "these [prophetic] stories . . . contain nearly all the accounts of miracles in the Hebrew Bible."[11]

The possible background for this emphasis on miracles, especially healings, is complex. There are at least three factors: the ancient widespread phenomenon of shamanism;[12] the more specific phenomenon in ancient Greece and the Near East of seer-healers;[13] and the further picture, yet more specific, of miracles done by God in the preceding part of the Primary History.

What matters most here is not the exact meaning of the emphasis on healing but simply its existence: it sets the Elijah-Elisha narrative apart and, to that extent, it indicates the narrative's unity.

Overall, therefore, these three unifying factors—succession, prophetic word, and healing—provide initial indications of the deliberateness with which the text has been constructed.

The full extent of that deliberateness becomes clearer when one examines a more basic factor: the structure.

A FULLER INDICATION OF UNITY: EIGHTFOLD STRUCTURE: TWO DRAMAS, EACH OF FOUR ACTS (OR DIPTYCHS)

The Elijah-Elisha narrative consists of two dramas, one centered on Elijah and his assumption (1 Kgs 16:29–2 Kgs 2:25), the other on Elisha and his burial (2 Kings 3–13). This distinction between orientation toward heaven and orientation toward burial is part of a larger complementarity: the Elijah account as a whole emphasizes human transcendence; the Elisha account, however, emphasizes human mortality, including the normal process of advancing from youth to old age.

Elijah almost seems above the restrictions of time and space. There is no allusion to his family or to his youth, and he never

---

[11] Thomas W. Overholt, *Cultural Anthropology and the Old Testament,* Guides to Biblical Scholarship (Minneapolis: Fortress Press, 1996) 24.

[12] Ibid., 30–50.

[13] Walter Burkert, *The Orientalizing Revolution: Near Eastern Influence on Greek Culture in the Early Archaic Age* (Cambridge, Mass.: Harvard University Press, 1992) 41–87.

seems to grow old. He arrives with the suddenness and power of God's word (1 Kgs 17:1); he breaks the barriers of space and speed (1 Kgs 18:12, 46); and he ascends in fire to heaven (2 Kings 2). A significant number of his actions take place on mountains: Carmel (1 Kgs 18:19-46), Horeb (1 Kgs 19:8-18), and an unnamed mountain (2 Kgs 1:9-15). Even Tishbe, his place of origin, was first understood as an uninhabited site in the mountains of Gilead.[14] Hence, while Elijah's life, particularly his confrontation with his own possible death (1 Kings 19), does indeed sometimes evoke life's visible progression, the overall emphasis is on highlighting another dimension: the vertical or transcendent.

Elisha, however, is just the reverse: while clearly involving the transcendent, he reflects the ordinary rhythm of life. The account of him is more like a biography, from childhood to grave. He does not linger on the mountains (2 Kgs 3:25), and, when he does, a distressed woman effectively asks him to come down (2 Kgs 4:25-30). The story of the woman's child contains a miniature birth narrative (2 Kgs 4:14-18) such as never occurs in the Elijah drama. Elisha himself is first presented as a strong young man who, having kissed his parents good-bye, accepts a form of apprenticeship with Elijah (1 Kgs 19:19-21). Later, as Elijah departs, Elisha's apprenticeship comes to fruition: he becomes a full prophet like his master (2 Kgs 2:1-18). But then just after he reaches this high point, small signs emerge of advancing years: he is *bald* (2 Kgs 2:23); he *breaks his journey* to eat and, later, to eat *and rest* (2 Kgs 4:8-10); he *has a house* of his own, in which he stays (2 Kgs 5:9-10) and to which he is later accompanied by *the elders* (2 Kgs 6:32). Then he is spoken of as if in the past (2 Kgs 8:4); *he weeps at the imminence of death* (2 Kgs 8:11); and he sends a *faster/younger man* in his own place (2 Kgs 9:1-3). Finally, like many old people, he *fades into the background* and is left unmentioned until he becomes terminally sick and someone comes and cries over him (1 Kgs 13:14). Then he dies, is buried, and is reduced to bones (2 Kgs 13:20-21).

---

[14] Marvin S. Sweeney, "Tishbite," *Harper's Bible Dictionary* (San Francisco: Harper & Row, 1985) 1078.

Taken together the two accounts form a double drama which expresses the two most basic dimensions of human life.

Each drama contains four acts. The first act, for instance, recounts the long drought (including the evil which leads into it: 1 Kgs 16:29–18:46). Each act may contain several scenes (or episodes), yet, whatever the number of scenes, the act is essentially twofold: like a two-part painting or diptych it contains two panels or texts which in various ways complement one another. The act concerning the drought, for example, consists essentially of the events surrounding the drought's beginning (1 Kgs 16:29–17:24), and, in the third year, the events surrounding its end (1 Kings 18). The beginning is formally announced at the opening of 1 Kings 17, and the end is effectively announced at the opening of 1 Kings 18. Despite a gap of three years, the beginning and end shape the act into two complementary parts. And so the Elijah-Elisha narrative goes on, eight complex acts, each divided into two basic complementary parts (see Table 1.1).[15]

The core of the two dramas deals with life and death. The beginning, despite its story of a drought, shows God's word as the Creator-like source of life. The subsequent acts portray the way the word engages life and, increasingly, death. During the first drama (1 Kgs 16:29–2 Kgs 2:25) the emphasis on death seems to increase, until it is turned back by Elijah's assumption into heaven. In the second drama, with the entrance of Jehu and Athaliah, death becomes almost overwhelming. But again, at the end, it is turned back. The word has accomplished its purpose.

In both dramas the progression of the four acts corresponds *in part* to the progressive stages of a human life. The opening acts (1 Kgs 16:29–18:46; 2 Kings 3–4), while describing negative events (infanticide, drought, war, famine), do not dwell on the negativity. Rather, they use it as a background to describe how God's word gives new life through the elements, through food, and especially to children.

The second acts (1 Kings 19–20; 2 Kings 5–8) show the prophets as continuing their mission, but with a touch of vulnerability:

[15] On the centrality of diptychs in Genesis, see T. L. Brodie, *Genesis as Dialogue: An Orientation Commentary. Literary, Historical and Theological* (New York/Oxford: Oxford University Press, forthcoming).

Elijah is afraid (1 Kgs 19:1-4) and Elisha, who shows signs of aging, weeps (2 Kgs 8:11). In both cases the vulnerability is connected with becoming aware of the shadow of death. The shadow is distant but real.

In the third acts (1 Kings 21–22; 2 Kings 9–10) death is no longer in the distance. It kills the best (Naboth) and the greatest (the king, Ahab), and, with Jehu, it sweeps through the land. In this act the two prophets, especially Elisha, are largely in the background.

The fourth acts (2 Kings 1–2; 11–13) recount the end in a chariot of fire and in a sickness that leads to the grave.

At every stage, though the shadow of death intensifies, there is also a sense of some greater form of life. Even Jehu's campaign is surrounded by God's prophetic word. At the end Elijah seems rejuvenated (2 Kings 1–2) and Elisha's death brings rejuvenation to others—to the dead man who rises up, and, in a sense, to the whole land (2 Kgs 13:14-25).

What is essential is that the accounts of these two prophets, despite their individuality, also contain reflections of some of the most basic features of life: life's two dimensions (transcendent and time-bound), and life's basic stages in relation to life and death.

THE SIGNIFICANCE OF TWO FOURS

The use of eight—two fours—as an organizing principle accords with other features of the Hebrew Scriptures. Four is a key indicator of completeness—the four winds, the four ends of the earth—and as such is central to biblical imagery. Four occurs in some basic texts, such as the four streams in Eden (Genesis 2), the fourfold camp in the desert (Numbers 2), and the fourfold vision of Ezekiel (Ezekiel 1). The effect of two fours, rather than just one, is to enhance and confirm the sense of completeness.

This organizing principle is found both on a very large scale and on a small scale. On a large scale it applies to the Hebrew Scriptures as a whole. David Noel Freedman, having analyzed the size and layout of the biblical books, summarizes: "The Hebrew Bible as we know it . . . consisted of two precisely symmetrical halves, which in turn were made up of four subsections . . . with

TABLE 1.1: THE EIGHT DIPTYCHS OF THE ELIJAH-ELISHA NARRATIVE

DRAMA ONE: ELIJAH

1. Drought and a Woman: Amid Evil, the Word Gives New Life (1 Kgs 16:29–18:46)

- Ahab, Jezebel: Evil. Drought begins. The word gives life (1 Kgs 16:29–17:24).
- Ahab, Jezebel: Killers. Drought will end. Carmel: more life, especially water (1 Kings 18).

2. Death Threatens (1 Kings 19–20)

- Jezebel threatens Elijah. Elijah, at Horeb, hears and revives. Purposeful return (1 Kings 19).
- Aram threatens Ahab. Ahab victorious but only half hears. Depressed return (1 Kings 20).

3. Death Comes Closer (1 Kings 21–22)

- Jezebel manipulates a lying court. Naboth murdered; punishment foretold (1 Kings 21).
- Spirit manipulates court prophets. Battle: Ahab killed; punishment fulfilled (1 Kings 22).

4. The Two Faces of Death: Fall and Assumption (2 Kings 1–2)

- Ahaziah's fall and illness: death as an implacable descent (2 Kings 1).
- Elijah's assumption: death as an ascent (2 Kings 2).

(Table 1.1 cont.)

DRAMA TWO: ELISHA

5. **War, Drought, Women: Amid Evil/Want, the Word Gives New Life** (2 Kings 3–4)
   - Warring king (in Moab). The Moabite king kills his son (2 Kings 3).
   - Women in want. The women save their sons (2 Kings 4).

6. **Arameans (Naaman; Hazael): Distant Shadows of Death** (2 Kings 5–8)
   - Naaman and Aramean raiders: hearing and seeing; not killing (2 Kgs 5:1–6:23).
   - Aramean invaders and Hazael: mishearing God, and not seeing; killing (2 Kgs 6:24–8:29).

7. **The Jehu: The Word Brings Death** (2 Kings 9–10)
   - Jehu kills three leaders: Israel's king; Judah's king; Jezebel (2 Kings 9).
   - Jehu kills three groups: Israel's royalty; Judah's royalty; Baalites (2 Kings 10).

8. **As Death Closes In: Temple-Based Restoration** (2 Kings 11–13)
   - Amid death, life within the Temple. Arms! Athaliah dies. King restored (2 Kings 11).
   - The Temple is renewed. Elisha's arms. Elisha dies. Israel restored (2 Kings 12–13).

a supplement . . . to make the numbers come out more evenly as well as inject yet another ingredient into the picture of totality and completeness."[16] On a small scale the principle is found, for instance, in the alphabetic or acrostic poems. There are just eight alphabetic poems; in the most elaborate of these, Psalm 119, each stanza contains eight lines, and the text centers on eight key words. Freedman explains: "The number 8 . . . as the companion of the number 7 in Ugaritic and biblical poetry (i.e., 7 // 7 + 1) . . . connotes completeness and totality and perfection and at the same time carries with it the connotations of the important number 4 (i.e., the four directions of the compass) only more so."[17] The structure of two fours, therefore, is not something rare or insignificant. It accords with a central concept of totality or completeness. As such it is well-suited to the Elijah-Elisha narrative's role of reflecting the entire Primary History and bringing it to completion.

Demonstrating this structure in detail would require a separate and substantial monograph. All that can be given here is a summary, an orientation, concerning the diptych nature of the eight acts.

DRAMA ONE: ELIJAH

ACT 1: THE GREAT DROUGHT (1 KGS 16:29–18:46)

The diptych's two parts (1 Kgs 16:29–17:24 // 1 Kings 18) not only announce the drought's beginning and end respectively (17:1; 18:1-2); they also complement one another in other ways. The evil of Ahab and Jezebel, for instance, pictured at the beginning of part one (16:29-33), reappears in more intense form within the beginning of part two: it now emerges that Ahab and Jezebel are not only evil; they are killers (18:4, 14).[18]

---

[16] D. N. Freedman, "The Symmetry of the Hebrew Bible," *ST* 46 (1992) 93.

[17] D. N. Freedman, *The Unity of the Hebrew Bible* (Ann Arbor: University of Michigan Press, 1991) 729.

[18] Incidentally, Elijah's killing of the prophets of Baal (1 Kgs 18:40), while not explicitly condemned, has negative associations. It is set near the beginning of the portrayal of Elijah, and, through its context (discovery,

There is complementarity also concerning basic elements of nature: God's power over water (1 Kings 17) is balanced on Mount Carmel by God's power over fire (1 Kings 18).

Other complementarities are of a more general kind. The second panel (1 Kings 18) is longer, both in its overall quantity and in its individual stories, and is more public.[19] Thus even within the first diptych there is a shift toward greater length and complexity. To some degree this shift toward complexity is not surprising: several features of human art tend toward increasing complexity, such as music or dance, or even displays of fireworks.

This move toward complexity helps to set the pattern for the whole Elijah-Elisha narrative: both within each diptych and within the narrative as a whole there is a tendency toward increasing length and complexity. Second panels are usually longer than first; and later stories are more continuous, especially in the Elisha accounts. For instance, while Elijah deals with just one woman, and briefly (1 Kgs 17:7-24), Elisha deals with two, and in a more complex way (2 Kgs 4:1-37). The Aramean wars go from occupying essentially just one chapter (1 Kings 20) to occupying almost three (2 Kings 6–8). Finally, in the story of Jehu and its aftermath there is a continuous account of four or five chapters (2 Kings 9–12 or 9–13; ch. 13 is loose).

---

fear, flight to the desert), has resonances of the initial murder committed by Moses, a murder which is implicitly condemned (Exod 2:11-15). Elijah's killing of the Baalites has similarities also to the later killing of the Baalites by Jehu, a murderer (2 Kgs 10:25). If Elijah's initial killing of the Baalites is to be linked with the initial murder committed by Moses, then it becomes part of a series of biblical texts which show several leading characters as having had murder in their hearts: David (2 Samuel 11), Paul (Acts 9:1), and Peter, who, like Judas, relies on the sword (John 18:10; cf. 18:2-3). This same feature—showing that a leading character, despite his goodness, contains the shadow of murder—may also provide part of the context for Elisha's initial cursing of the mocking boys, a curse which effectively leads to death (2 Kgs 2:23-25). Curiously, the account of Elisha's curse mentions Mount Carmel (2 Kgs 2:25), the place where Elijah first ordered the killing (1 Kgs 18:40). This adds plausibility to the idea of some link or continuity between Elijah's command to kill and Elisha's deathly curse.

[19] Walsh, *1 Kings,* 236.

What is important for the moment is the complementarity within the first diptych (1 Kgs 16:29–17:24 // 1 Kings 18): the difference between the drought's simple beginning and its more complex end does not destroy the diptych's basic unity. Rather, it sets the tone for much of what is to come.

ACT 2: FROM DEATH THREATS TO TEMPORARY SURVIVAL (1 KINGS 19–20)

Part one (ch. 19) of this diptych is relatively private: Elijah, threatened by Jezebel, flees. However, within this privacy there are interventions: he is met by an angel in the desert and by God at Horeb; he returns to call Elisha.

Part two (ch. 20) is more public: Ben-haded of Aram threatens Ahab with overwhelming war, and, in effect, with death. However, here too there are interventions: a prophet (20:13, 22) and a man of God (20:28) turn the war around. In the end Ahab mishandles the victory—Ben-haded buys him off—and so Ahab returns depressed.

Both Elijah and Ahab are saved from death, but only for a time. In calling Elisha as successor, Elijah effectively acknowledges his mortality. And Ahab, despite his victory, is condemned to eventual death (20:42). The crucial difference between Elijah and Ahab is that, when faced by divine intervention, Elijah manages to absorb the divine word, but Ahab, though apparently receptive at first, does not. 1 Kings 19 ends with purposeful energy; chapter 20 with angry depression.

There are a number of minor complementarities between the texts, but the clearest is at the beginning, in the issuing of the threat:

> 19:2: "Jezebel sent a messenger to Elijah saying, 'May the gods do this to me . . . if by this time tomorrow . . .'"

> 20:1-6: "Ben-haded . . . sent messengers to Ahab . . . and the messengers came again and said . . . '. . . This time tomorrow I will send . . .'"

Obviously the latter threat, that of Ben-haded (20:1-6), is more elaborate. This accords with the overall proportions of the two parts: chapter 20 is twice the length of chapter 19. It also accords with the opening diptych's (1 Kgs 16:29–18:46) tendency toward greater length and complexity. Both panels follow a basic three-part arrangement:

- A preliminary encounter: an angel directs threatened Elijah to eat and walk (19:1-8) and a prophet directs the threatened king to organize and attack (20:1-25).

- A climactic encounter: at Horeb, YHWH's appearance enables Elijah to face apparently overwhelming odds (19:9-18); at Aphek YHWH, "god of the mountains," enables Israel to overcome overwhelming odds (20:26-34).

- The denouement: leaving the mountain, Elijah comes and calls Elisha (19:19-21); Ahab, on his way back, is met by a reproaching prophet (20:35-43).

In the denouement the relationship between the texts is one of acute contrast. The Elijah/Elisha scene (19:19-21) is concise and full of freedom and vitality: plowing, twelve yoke of oxen, Elisha's closeness to the oxen, Elijah's apparent gentleness in calling him, running, kissing, slaughtering for cooking, eating, and, finally, as he embraces discipleship, Elisha's purposeful departure from home: "and he arose and followed after Elijah and attended him." The Ahab scene (20:35-43), however, is highly negative: striking, killing, wounding, condemning, and, finally, Ahab's journey home: "and the king . . . went back . . . sullen and angry."

Taken together the two panels (chs. 19 and 20) not only dramatize God's saving intervention, they also highlight the contrast between the one who fully accepts God's word and the one who does not.

ACT 3: NABOTH'S MURDER AND ITS PUNISHMENT (1 KINGS 21–22)

The two panels of this act or diptych tell respectively of the murder of Naboth (1 Kings 21) and the subsequent death of Ahab in battle (1 Kings 22). The two events—Naboth's murder and Ahab's death—are closely linked: one is a punishment for the other. When Naboth is murdered, Elijah announces that in the place where the dogs licked Naboth's blood they will lick Ahab's blood also (21:19). And later, when Ahab's bloodied chariot was washed, the dogs did so "as the word . . . had spoken" (22:38). The second part therefore refers back explicitly to the first, fulfilling it. As with the drought, the two panels of the diptych are essentially three years apart (22:1; cf. 18:1).

Following the pattern of earlier diptychs, the second panel (1 Kings 22) is longer, more elaborate, and more public; it involves kings, complex courts, and armies. The chapter on Naboth is relatively private; most of the account involves just two characters: Ahab and Naboth, Ahab and Jezebel, YHWH and Elijah, Elijah and Ahab (21:1-7, 17-29).

However, within the Naboth text one episode is very public: the central account of the court that condemned him to death (21:8-16). It is a court dominated by the lies of false witnesses.

This lie-dominated court of chapter 21 provides a compact counterpart for the elaborate lie-dominated courts of chapter 22: the assembly of about four hundred false prophets, gathered before the kings (22:5-12), and the heavenly assembly in which a lying spirit undertakes to speak through the false prophets (22:19-23). The corruption of the word at the judicial level (in the Naboth case) is balanced by corruption at the prophetic level (the false prophets).

In contrast to these lying courts, both panels present fearless prophets who genuinely represent YHWH and who immediately confront Ahab: Elijah confronts him as he takes possession of Naboth's vineyard (20:16-24), and Micaiah confronts him as he seeks to take possession of Ramoth-gilead (22:15-17).

Thus the diptych as a whole deals not only with Naboth's murder and its punishment, but also with the lying distortion of the word and with the true prophets who in diverse ways confront the distortion.

ACT 4: AHAZIAH'S FALL AND ELISHA'S ASSUMPTION
(2 KINGS 1–2)

This diptych tells of two people, a king and a prophet, who both departed from this life. But their ways of departing were very diverse. The king, Ahaziah, fell from his upper room and died without ever rising from his bed (2 Kings 1). The prophet, Elijah, crossed the Jordan and was taken up to heaven (2 Kings 2). The essential contrast, or complementarity, is between a fall and an ascent.

Both departures are accompanied by the prophetic word. Ahaziah dies in accordance with the repeated word of YHWH (2 Kgs 1:4, 7, 16, 17). Elijah's departure is likewise in accordance with the prophetic word and YHWH's command (2 Kgs 2:1, 3, 5).

The contrast between the king and the prophet is already implicit in 2 Kings 1: while the fallen king is confined to bed, Elijah is found to be seated on an unnamed mountain (*har,* 2 Kgs 2:9). The Hebrew verb for going up the mountain (*ʾālâ,* "go up/ascend," 2 Kgs 1:9) is the same as for Elijah's going up to heaven (2 Kgs 2:11).

While on this unnamed mountain Elijah *calls down fire from heaven* (2 Kgs 1:10, 12; cf. 1:14); in the next chapter he himself is *borne away to heaven in a chariot of fire* (2 Kgs 2:11). Thus, there is also a complementarity of descent and ascent concerning the fire. As Elijah on the mountain is approached three times by groups of fifty men (2 Kgs 1:9, 11, 13), so also, but in a very different way, Elijah's ascent is accompanied by the presence of various groups of fifty (2 Kgs 2:7, 16, 17).

In contrast to earlier diptychs, where second-panel events were plainly public, the second panel in this case is more complex. The taking up of Elijah (2 Kings 2) may indeed seem to be public—he ascends dramatically in a chariot of fire—yet his ascent is surrounded by a cloak of prophets' hushed speech. His departure is thoroughly verified, both before and after (2 Kgs 2:1-7, 15-18), but only Elisha, who walks with him, even across the Jordan, actually sees him going (2 Kgs 2:8-12).[20]

---

[20] Two details: The repeated references to Moab's rebellion (2 Kgs 1:1; 3:4-5) may perhaps be a further factor, a kind of envelope or *inclusio,* in binding together the two panels (2 Kings 1–2). And as mentioned above (n. 17), Elisha's fatal cursing of the boys (2 Kgs 2:23-25) may be part of a pattern of biblical texts which indicate the murderous shadow even of good people, including Elijah.

The essence of the two panels is that they show two complementary faces of death. Ahaziah's fate shows death as a descent: a banal accident leaves him in bed critically ill and, having placed his faith in false gods, his destiny is to stay in bed and die. Elijah's passing, however, is a mystery-filled ascent.

DRAMA TWO: ELISHA

ACT 5: THE WATER, THE WOMAN, AND THE SON
(2 KINGS 3–4)

Following Elijah's ascent the focus switches to Elisha; first to his involvement in the terrible Moabite war (2 Kings 3), then to his role with women, children, and food (2 Kings 4).

At first sight the two panels of this diptych seem unrelated: war and women. But a closer look shows significant continuity.

First of all, the diptych as a whole (2 Kings 3–4) builds considerably on the initial Elijah diptych (1 Kgs 16:29–18:46). Apart from the obvious links concerning the women/widows, oil, and sons (1 Kgs 17:7-24; cf. 2 Kgs 4:1-37), there is a basic continuity concerning the lack of water: the image of drought that overshadows the beginning of the Elijah account reappears in modified form in the Moabite war. The three invading kings (of Israel, Judah, and Edom) are left without water, and the intervention of Elisha, who effectively commands the water (2 Kgs 3:14-17), has echoes of the initial intervention of Elijah (1 Kgs 17:1-3). Altogether, the account of the Moabite war refers to water seven times (2 Kgs 3:9, 11, 17, 18, 20, 22, 25).

What is essential is that the beginning of the Elijah account (esp. 1 Kings 17) provides an initial clue to the unity of the beginning of the Elisha account, 2 Kings 3–4. Elements that are bound closely together in 1 Kings 17 are dispersed in 2 Kings 3–4.

With regard to the relationship between the two panels themselves (between 2 Kings 3 and 4), the gap is not as wide as it seems at first. The emphasis on water (2 Kings 3) provides an understandable counterpart to the emphasis on women, children, and food (2 Kings 4). Unlike war, with its harvest of destruction and death, all four of these elements—water, women, children, food—are essentially positive, life-giving. As already partly indicated, all four elements were bound together in 1 Kings 17.

Furthermore, these two chapters (2 Kings 3 and 4) are also joined by something more specific: the climactic emphasis on endangered sons. The Moabite war ends with the Moabite king sacrificing his eldest son (2 Kgs 3:24). The women in 2 Kings 4, however, the widow and the Shunammitess, do the opposite: they are concerned with saving their sons. The Shunammitess, far from killing her son, effectively has him brought back to life (2 Kgs 4:32-37).

This climactic emphasis on the fate of the sons is a development not only of 1 Kings 17 but also of the introductory reference to how Hiel of Bethel rebuilt Jericho at the cost of his two sons (1 Kgs 16:34).

What is important, however, is the basic link, or rather contrast, between chapters 3 and 4. The Moabite war—total devastation culminating in infanticide—is like a terrible foil for the life-giving episodes of 2 Kings 4, including the final stories about soup and bread (2 Kgs 4:38-44).

This diptych shows complementary aspects of Elisha, and implicitly of God. God punishes haughty kings (2 Kings 3); God also cares for the poor or deprived (2 Kings 4). There is some small but significant affinity here with the Bible's first two creation texts: Genesis 1 and 2, whatever one's view of their origin, effectively highlight diverse aspects of God.

This diptych also contains complementary portrayals of men (2 Kings 3) and women (2 Kings 4). Overall, the Elijah-Elisha narrative does not give prominence to women, and its description of Jezebel is deadly. But on this occasion (chs. 3–4) its portrayal of women, both poor and rich, is resoundingly positive. While the men are drawn into boasting and destructive war, even infanticide, the women, despite their impoverishment of one kind or another (indebtedness or barrenness), are acting positively to make the best of what they have. They seek help, they offer help, and they do all they can to help their children. The man-woman contrast is particularly acute in the story of the Shunammitess: when the child is in crisis the man is helpless, but the woman is receptive and decisive (2 Kgs 4:18-24).

ACT 6: ARAM'S EXPERIENCE: TWO SIDES OF GOD'S ACTION
(2 KINGS 5–8)

This four-chapter diptych is distinguished by its emphasis on Aram and Aram's king. The first verse introduces Naaman and presents him as commander to Aram's king (5:1). The main final episode tells how Aram's king died (8:7-15). The implication throughout is that the king is Ben-haded, but his name is not used until 6:24, the beginning of the siege of Samaria as well as the beginning of the diptych's second part.

The diptych's six main episodes form two clusters of three:

- Naaman the leper, faithful commander to Aram's king (2 Kings 5).
- Finding the borrowed axe (6:1-7).
- Raiding Arameans, led into Samaria, are sent home (6:8-23).

- Invading Arameans at Samaria; lepers find good news (6:24–7:20).
- Restoring the Shunammitess's property (8:1-6).
- In Damascus; Hazael, treacherous aide to Aram's king (8:7-15).

The division between the two parts (5:1–6:23 // 6:24–8:29) is stark. Part one ends by saying that Aramean raiders stopped attacking Israel (6:23). Part two begins by showing the Arameans attacking Israel in force (6:24). Apparently part of the reason for the seeming contradiction is precisely to divide the diptych in two.

As far as details are concerned, the two panels/parts of the diptych have multiple correspondences. More specifically, the three episodes of panel one (5:1–6:23) resonate in diverse ways through panel two (6:24–8:29).

EPISODE ONE: NAAMAN (2 KINGS 5)

Distinct elements of this leper's story reappear in the account of the siege of Samaria: leprosy; silver, gold, and clothing; Elisha in his own house sending/receiving a messenger; the king leaning on the arm of the commander/officer; the punishment of the person (Gehazi/the officer) who misuses or despises the prophetic word (6:32; 7:3, 8, 17, 20).

EPISODE TWO: FINDING THE BORROWED AXE (2 KGS 6:1-7)

Insofar as this story implies the importance of restoring property, it prepares for the more elaborate account of restoring property to the Shunammitess (2 Kgs 8:1-6).

These two short episodes—the lost axe and the return of the Shunammitess—are a good example of narratives that are hugely different, each with its own immediate context and social world, but that nonetheless share a basic concern, in this case restoration.

EPISODE THREE: ARAMEAN RAIDERS ARE LED INTO SAMARIA (2 KGS 6:8-23)

This serves in part to prepare for the larger Aramean siege of Samaria (6:24–7:20). For instance, compare the pictures of a perplexed king being advised by his servants (6:11-14; 7:12-15).

The pivotal element of the Naaman story—the dipping (*tābal,* "bathe/dip") that led to a form of rebirth (5:14)—finds a contrasting echo in the dipping *(tābal)* that led to the death of Ben-haded (8:15).

Aspects of the first panel (5:1–6:23) are quite public, but the second panel (6:24–8:29) is public on a grander scale. The second-panel scenes generally are more open and the frame of reference broader, even as regards time and space. Thus something of the private/public complementarity that occurs in the Elijah drama occurs here also, but more elaborately.

The central complementarity between the two panels concerns diverse responses to the word. In panel one, the Arameans learn to hear and see (Naaman hears; the blinded warriors see). In panel two, however, the Aramean invaders neither hear nor see: they mishear the God-given noise (literally, voice) and they flee into the darkness (2 Kgs 8:6-7, 15). Correspondingly, panel one concludes with an emphasis on not killing (2 Kgs 6:21-22), and panel two with a picture of murder (Hazael, the antithesis of Naaman, kills his master; 2 Kgs 8:14-15).

The deathly consequences of not being receptive to God's life-giving word are also seen in the fate of the cynical officer who is trodden to death (2 Kgs 7:2, 16-20).

Some further sense of the diptych's basic theme emerges from an apparently casual detail. The story of restoring the Shunammitess refers puzzlingly to the intermediary role of Gehazi (2 Kgs 8:4-5), the man otherwise known largely through his greed in the Naaman episode and last seen as a leper, someone who was literally on the way out (2 Kgs 5:20-27; cf. 2 Kgs 4:25-32). His reappearance here confirms the diptych structure—he intervenes once in each panel—but there is no reference now (in 2 Kings 8) to his leprosy. Far from being outside or isolated, as lepers sometimes were, he is introduced as being inside, as conversing easily with the king, telling him stories about the prophet Elisha.

This apparent contradiction between Gehazi's exclusion and inclusion is purposeful. The leprosy is not denied; and the apparent leper's easy relationship with the king corresponds to Naaman's relationship to *his* king: the army commander, despite his leprosy, was first introduced precisely as highly regarded by his king (2 Kgs 5:1).

The other lepers in the diptych, the four who apparently were isolated (alone between the city and the besieging army), are in the odd position of knowing far more than the king (2 Kgs 7:3-15). They bring good news, thus fulfilling the prophetic word, while the king and his horses still grope in the dark.

Thus in the diptych as a whole, the portrayal of lepers, despite its diversity, has a basic consistency. Leprosy may be terrible, something variously seen as a malady which God wants to heal (Naaman), as a punishment (Gehazi), or as causing isolation (the four outside the city). But people who bear that malady are close to the king (Naaman, Gehazi) or close to the prophetic word (the four, Gehazi). Thus the final brief picture of Gehazi telling life-giving prophetic stories to the king is like a synthesis of what earlier leper stories had implied: leprosy does not mean exclusion. If Gehazi's leprosy is not mentioned in this final picture (2 Kgs 8:4-6) it is because, in the final analysis, the leprosy does not count.

Act 7: Jehu (2 Kings 9–10)

The Elijah-Elisha narrative now enters its final and most continuous phase: an essentially unbroken sequence of four or five chapters (2 Kings 9–12 or 9–13; as already noted, ch. 13 is attached, but loosely). In contrast to the succession of short episodes that make up the beginning of the Elijah story (1 Kings 17), this final sequence gives the narrative a new shape. But the new shape, the new continuity, does not disrupt the steady diptych structure. The Jehu chapters (2 Kings 9–10) constitute one diptych; the final chapters (2 Kings 11–13) constitute another.

The action begins when Elisha sends one of the prophetic brotherhood to anoint Jehu (2 Kgs 9:1-3). This task was originally assigned at Horeb to Elijah (1 Kgs 19:16), but it was given in conjunction with the initial fading of Elijah and with the choosing of Elisha to succeed him (1 Kgs 19:16). Responsibility therefore falls to Elisha. However, the anointing of Jehu requires speed, especially in getting away after the event (2 Kings 1, 3, 10), and Elisha sends someone who can move fast (2 Kgs 9:1).

Jehu's revolt has two distinct phases. Panel one (2 Kings 9) describes the initial high-speed takeover that kills three leading individuals: the two kings and Jezebel. Panel two (2 Kings 10) tells of the more deliberate process of eliminating three leading groups: members of the two royal houses and the Baalites. The three groups correspond essentially to the three individuals:

2 Kings 9	2 Kings 10
Jehu's accession (9:1-21)	———
Israel's king (9:22-26)	Israel's royal family (10:1-11)
Judah's king (9:27-29)	Brothers of Judah's king (10:12-14)
Jezebel (9:30-37)	Baalites (10:18-27)
———	Jehu's reign (10:28-36)

A detail helps to pin down the correspondence between the panels. The final reference to the remains of Jezebel ("like dung/manure/waste," *dōmen,* 9:37) is echoed at the end of the Baalite text: their demolished Temple became a latrine (10:27).

Jehu's accession is a whirlwind affair with running, shouts of acclamation, and the spreading of cloaks on the ground. And after his terrible purging is over, especially his climactic destruction of the Temple (2 Kgs 10:20-27), the summary of his reign praises him, initially at least, for what he has done (2 Kgs 10:28-30).

What is essential for the moment is the unity and structure: the account of Jehu's purging of Israel's leaders and Temple (2 Kings 9–10) consists, as do previous texts, of a diptych. The difference between individuals (ch. 9) and groups (ch. 10) corresponds broadly to the difference noted in other diptychs between private and public. However, for the first and only time, in this case the second panel (ch. 10, with 36 verses) is not significantly longer than the first (ch. 9, with 37 verses). The relative brevity of the second panel may, perhaps, have something to do with its deathly content.

ACT 8: AFTER THE TEMPLE DEVELOPMENT: ARMS, DEATH, AND RESTORATION (2 KINGS 11–13)

The final diptych, still feeling the effects of Jehu's coup, begins with Athaliah's elimination of the royal house of Judah, yet the diptych as a whole is positive, a portrayal of restoration.

The first part (2 Kings 11) tells how, despite Athaliah's mass murder, there was a secret development in the Temple: a sole surviving baby, Joash, was nurtured for six years (11:1-3). Then, in the seventh year, there was a dramatic sequence of events: a call to arms (11:4-12), the death of Athaliah (11:13-16), and the covenant-based restoration of the king (11:17-20).

All of these events are echoed in the diptych's second part (2 Kings 12–13), but on a scale that is more elaborate or more distant:

Boy develops in Temple (11:1-3)	Caring for the Temple (ch. 12)
Call to arms (11:4-12)	Ill Elisha calls to arms (13:14-19)
Death of Athaliah (11:13-16)	Death of Elisha (13:20-21)
Covenant-based restoration (11:17-20)	Covenant-based restoration (13:22-25)

The emphasis on the Jerusalem Temple, unique in the Elijah-Elisha narrative, occurs clearly in both panels of the diptych, but instead of tending to a child within the Temple (11:1-3) there is a more elaborate account of tending to the Temple itself (ch. 12). The call to arms by Jehoida the priest, who commands the soldiers and supplies them with weapons, finds a complement in the scene of Elisha's illness: in the commands, the hands, the weapons (chariot, horsemen, bow, arrows; 13:14-19). The details here are complex. To some degree the words of the king beside sick Elisha are an exact echo of Elisha's own words beside departing Elijah ("My father! My father! Chariots of Israel and its horsemen!" 2 Kgs 2:12; 13:14). But when Elisha, partly reflecting Elijah, then imparts some of his strength to the king, he does so in a way that is both a call to arms ("Take bow and arrows," 13:15) and a mission ("You will destroy Aram . . . ," 13:17).

The inglorious death of Athaliah, who rends her garments and is expelled from the Temple (11:13-16), finds an enigmatic complementary contrast in the wondrous death of Elisha—in the way his bones raise a dead man (13:20-21). This contrast between the death of Queen Athaliah and that of Elisha (2 Kings 11 and 13) builds partly on the earlier contrast between the death/fate of King Ahaziah and that of Elijah (2 Kings 1 and 2).

Finally, the covenant-making which led to the restoration of the king (11:19-20) finds a climactic complement in the account of how YHWH, because of the covenant with Abraham, Isaac, and Jacob, enabled the king to defeat Aram and restore the cities of Israel (13:22-25).

Taken as a whole this diptych gives the Elijah-Elisha narrative a crowning emphasis on the Temple; yet the final episode, the death of Elisha (13:14-25) moves the focus to a wider horizon, to the defeating of death and the restoration of Israel's cities.

The final chapter, 2 Kings 13, especially Elisha's death and its consequences (13:14-25), is curiously loose. At one level it does indeed fit well into the diptych; its elements correspond to elements in panel one (ch. 11). But at another level, that of narrative sequence, it is surprising. It is surprising, first of all, in its details; some say it is confusing, thus leading to "numerous attempts to 'improve' the order of the verses."[21] It is surprising also in its basic content. So many chapters had made no mention of Elisha that he seemed to have faded from the narrative. Now suddenly he is back. It is to him apparently that chapter 13 refers when it speaks of Yhwh having sent "a deliverer" (13:5).[22] And then he is mentioned explicitly: his illness, his life-giving death, and the subsequent restoration of Israel's cities (13:14-25).

The reintroduction of Elisha has two basic effects. On the one hand it ties the whole sequence of 2 Kings 9–13 into a unity. It was Elisha who set that sequence in motion when he sent someone to anoint Jehu—in fact, the sequence even begins with his name (9:1)—and so it is appropriate that he too should close it. On the other hand, the nature of the closing is so loose and surprising, even disruptive, that it suggests there is more to history than smooth sequences. The disruptive surprise reaches a high point when, after Elisha dies, his bones bring a dead man back to life (13:20-21).

What is essential again is that amid the text's diversity, including its stark surprises, the basic unity and structure are maintained. The whole of 2 Kings 9–13 forms a single prolonged sequence, and within that sequence the narrative is organized in diptychs.

Summary Features

It is useful at this stage to summarize some general features of the eight diptychs.

The number of verses in the several diptychs is as follows:

The Elijah drama: 30/46 21/43 29/54 18/25 Total = 266

The Elisha drama: 27/44 50/59 37/36 20/47 Total = 320

Within each diptych the second part/panel is generally longer, and, taking the Elijah-Elisha narrative as a whole, the second drama concerning Elisha is also longer.

[21] Richard Nelson, *First and Second Kings,* Interpretation (Atlanta: John Knox Press, 1987) 215.

[22] Paul House, *1, 2 Kings,* New American Commentary (Nashville: Broadman & Holman, 1995) 306.

Lengthy formulaic passages (summaries of reigns according to standard formulae) are generally not placed in the middle of diptychs. They usually occur either at the diptych's beginning or, more often, at its conclusion:

Beginnings: 1 Kgs 16:29-34; 2 Kgs 3:1-3

Conclusions: 1 Kgs 22:39-54; 2 Kgs 8:16-29; 10:28-36

These formulaic conclusions add further to the second part of several diptychs.

This general rule of no formulaic passages in the middle has one notable exception: the last diptych (2 Kings 11–13). Here the formulae occur both in introducing the reign of Joash (12:1-4) and especially before the death of Elisha (13:1-13). This unusual arrangement allows the narrative to end not with a largely-predictable formula but on an appropriately significant note: the wondrous death of Elisha and the covenant-based restoration of the cities.

GENERAL CONCLUSION TO CHAPTER 1

The evidence for the unity of the Elijah-Elisha narrative is considerable: correspondence to a succession narrative, cohesion around the central dynamic of the (prophetic) word, unique emphasis on healing, and a coherent eightfold diptych structure.

This brief sketch of the diptych structure of the Elijah-Elisha narrative does not show the details of that structure, but it does do something basic for it: it indicates that it exists. At the very least, it shows that the idea of an eightfold diptych structure is a worthwhile working hypothesis.

CHAPTER 2

A SYNTHESIS OF
THE PRIMARY HISTORY:
INITIAL COMPARISON

ANOTHER KIND OF RELATIONSHIP

The preceding chapter has shown some of the internal relationships between the texts of the Elijah-Elisha narrative, particularly the relationships within the diptychs. But, like people, texts
can combine diverse relationships. A person with strong internal
relationships, such as with family or friends, can also have strong
outside relationships. One can be close to a sister and also work
as foreign minister (secretary of state). A text with a strong affinity to the other panel of its diptych or to another part or the Elijah-
Elisha narrative can also interact with an outside text.

The texts within the Elijah-Elisha narrative are subtly complex[1] and have at least two basic kinds of relationships. The internal relationships are with the other parts of a diptych and with the
Elijah-Elisha narrative as a whole; the external, with a distant part
of the larger Primary History. The journey of threatened Elijah to
Horeb (1 Kings 19) is in diptych relationship with the invasion
that threatens Ahab (1 Kings 20), but it also reflects the more distant history of Moses (Exodus-Deuteronomy).

---

[1] Patricia Dutcher-Walls, *Narrative Art, Political Rhetoric: The Case
of Athaliah and Joash,* JSOTSS 209 (Sheffield: Sheffield Academic,
1996) 180–7.

Given this twofold relationship—internal and external—it is possible to conclude that a specific text, such as the basic Elijah story, is somehow dependent both on preceding texts/traditions of the Primary History and also on other texts/traditions of the Elijah-Elisha narrative itself.[2] As a literary conclusion this is essentially true, yet it is but part of a larger truth, namely that all the Elijah-Elisha texts entail two kinds of relationships.

The main thesis of this brief book is that the Elijah-Elisha narrative, as well as having an eightfold diptych structure, also reflects the rest of the Primary History (Genesis-Kings); thus, it contains at least two basic kinds of relationships.

These two sets of relationships, internal and external, do not follow the same structure. While the diptych structure is eightfold—no more, no less—the relationship to the large outside text is inherently subject to more variation; in principle it can be divided in diverse ways. (While one's sibling/family relationships are generally stable, relationships to the complex outside world can vary enormously.) In this case, rather than divide the external relationship into eight, it seems more appropriate to divide it into ten. Apparently, for practical purposes, the composer of the Elijah-Elisha narrative divided the entire rest of the Primary History into about ten blocks and then reshaped them so that they contributed to an orderly eightfold narrative.

Many of these blocks consist of one book—Genesis, Joshua, Judges, 1 Samuel, and 2 Samuel. But the four books dealing with the life of Moses apparently have been treated as a unit, one narrative block. On the other hand 1 and 2 Kings, the final books, have been subdivided, each into two blocks. The details become clearer in the process of comparison.

THE INITIAL COMPARISON

On the left of Table 2.1 (under "Genesis-Kings") is an essentially straightforward list of the eleven books from Genesis to

---

[2] Marsha White, *The Elijah Legends and Jehu's Coup,* Brown Judaic Studies 311 (Atlanta: Scholars Press, 1997) 3–31.

2 Kings. The next column lists at least one of that book's leading events. For example, "Flood" is listed next to "Genesis," since the flood is one of Genesis' most striking and significant events. Likewise with the four books which begin and end with Moses (Exodus-Deuteronomy), many of their leading events occur at Sinai/Horeb. Each book, whatever its complexity, has some event or events, often near the beginning, which stand out. In the case of David (2 Samuel) one of the most striking events is his affair with Bathsheba: David's seeing her from the roof, and the conception of their child. For Solomon (1 Kings 1–11) a primary eye-catching moment is the visit of the Queen of Sheba.

The right side of Table 2.1 lists the main events in the Elijah-Elisha narrative. Two features are important—content and order:

CONTENT

The events of the Elijah-Elisha narrative correspond in basic ways to the striking events of the larger history. While Genesis' first prolonged drama is a flood, Elijah's first great drama is a drought. The two (flood/drought) are like opposite sides of the same coin, both illustrating God's primordial power over the elements, especially over water.

When, after Genesis, the Primary History switches its focus to Sinai/Horeb, Elijah does likewise: he walks, Moses-like, for forty days, to meet God at Horeb. And when, after Moses, Joshua *undertakes invasion* (besieging Jericho), the Elijah-Elisha narrative recounts how Israel had to *endure invasion* (the siege of Samaria) —again two sides of the same coin (invading/being invaded), both illustrating God's power.

The rest of the Elijah-Elisha narrative follows essentially the same pattern. The vivid account near the beginning of Judges— how Deborah took over and Jael killed—is refracted in the story of Naboth: Jezebel in effect took over and killed (1 Kings 21).

The prophecies and wars of 1 Samuel, culminating in the death of Saul in battle, are variously mirrored through Ahab's death in battle and through the subsequent account of prophets and wars (2 Kings 1–3).

TABLE 2.1: THE MIRRORING OF GENESIS-KINGS IN ELIJAH-ELISHA: A MINIMUM OUTLINE

GENESIS-KINGS		THE ELIJAH-ELISHA NARRATIVE	
(EXCEPT 1 KGS 16:29–2 KGS 13:25)		(1 KGS 16:29–2 KGS 13:25)	
Genesis-Kings	*Leading Episode(s)*	*1 Kgs 16:29–2 Kgs 13:25*	*Main Episode(s)*
Genesis	Flood	1 Kings 17–18	Drought
Exodus-Deuteronomy	Sinai/Horeb	1 Kings 19	Horeb
Joshua	Siege of Jericho; Ai	1 Kings 20	Siege of Samaria; Aphek
Judges	Deborah takes over; Jael kills	1 Kings 21	Naboth: Jezebel takes over, to kill
1 Samuel	Saul: Prophets, wars, Saul dies	1 Kings 22–2 Kings 3	Ahab dies; prophets; wars
2 Samuel	David on roof; woman conceives	2 Kings 4	Prophet on roof; woman conceives
1 Kings 1–11	Queen of Sheba	2 Kings 5	Naaman
1 Kings 12–16	Schismatic war; prophecy	2 Kings 6–8	War and prophetic power
2 Kings 14–17	Israel's murders and fall	2 Kings 9–10	Jehu murders the house of Israel
2 Kings 18–25	Hezekiah thwarts death; Josiah's reform, end	2 Kings 11–13	Joash's reform; Elisha's death leads to new life; end

Instead of David's affair, beginning on the roof, there is the story of the prophet who, welcomed to the roof by a dignified woman, enables her to conceive (2 Kings 4). Instead of the foreign queen who came from afar to hear the wisdom of Israel and see its wealth, there is Naaman, commander to a foreign monarch, who came with wealth to Israel and discovered the power of the simple word of the prophet (2 Kings 5).

Soon after the visit of the queen of Sheba, the text of 1 Kings recounts a schismatic war which highlights the role of the prophet (1 Kings 12–16). The Elijah-Elisha narrative correspondingly tells of Aramean wars in which the role of the prophet is even clearer (2 Kings 6–8).

Thus, up to 2 Kings 8, the Elijah-Elisha text mirrors what precedes.

Then (2 Kings 9–13) it mirrors what follows (2 Kings 14–25). Instead of the complex account of Israel's assassinations and eventual fall (2 Kings 14–17) the Elijah-Elisha narrative gives the single dramatic story of Jehu—his assassinations and his destruction of the house of Israel (2 Kings 9–10).

Finally, the account of the end of the Jerusalem kingship (2 Kings 18–25) supplies an important part of the Jerusalem-centered conclusion of the Elisha story (2 Kings 11–13). Josiah's reform (chs. 22–23) inspires the account of the reform of Joash (chs. 11–12), and Hezekiah's recovery from deathly illness (chs. 18–20, esp. 20) contributes to the account of Elisha's extraordinary illness and death (ch. 13).

At the very end both accounts suggest a process of restoration. The Primary History, having recounted the Babylonian invasion and the death-filled fall of Jerusalem (23:31–25:26), hints, in its low-key picture of the king's pardon and elevation (25:27-30), that events are moving toward some form of restoration or recovery. The Elijah-Elisha narrative, having alluded very briefly to a form of death and invasion (Elisha's death and the Moabites' invasion, 13:20), then recounts not only recovery from death (13:21) but also—and quite clearly—Israel's restoration (the restoration of its cities, 13:22-25). This latter restoration is not something casual. It is based on nothing less than God's original covenant with Abraham, Isaac, and Jacob. Thus the very end of the Elijah-Elisha narrative manages not only to clarify the idea of restoration that occurs at the Primary History's conclusion, but also to recall the covenant at the History's beginning.

Overall, therefore, the content of the Elijah-Elisha narrative corresponds significantly to that of the entire Primary History. The Elisha-Elisha narrative places a far greater emphasis on prophecy, yet its events—the elements of its plot—are strikingly akin to those of the larger history.

ORDER

As Table 2.1 indicates, the order of the events in the Elijah-Elisha narrative matches that of the Primary History. As a general principle, similarity of order does not come easily. If two people are asked to set five random elements in order, the chance that they will follow the same order is less than one in one hundred. With ten elements, the chance is less than one in a million.

If, however, one sees the work of the other, then following the same order is easy.

The implication is more than a million to one: the author of the Elijah-Elisha narrative saw the near-complete Primary History and followed its order.

QUANTITY ANALYSIS: SPIRALING PROPORTIONS

One of the features of the way the Elijah-Elisha narrative mirrors the rest of the Primary History is the variation of proportions. Events in the pre-monarchical period (Genesis-Judges) are greatly reduced, but monarchical times loom larger. There is in fact a kind of sliding scale:

Genesis: reduced to about two chapters (1 Kgs 16:29–18:46).

***

Exodus-Deuteronomy: reduced to one chapter (1 Kings 19).

Joshua: reduced to one chapter (1 Kings 20).

Judges: reduced to one chapter (1 Kings 21).

1 Samuel: reduced to four chapters (1 Kings 22–2 Kings 3)

***

2 Samuel: reduced to one chapter (2 Kings 4).

1 Kings 1–16: reduced to three chapters (2 Kings 5–8)

2 Kings 14–25: reduced to five chapters (2 Kings 9–13).

Genesis, presumably because of its pride of place, does relatively well. Even though it is the most distant or ancient-looking of all, it receives about two chapters.

After that there is a spiraling gradation. First there is a progression from the intense reduction imposed on Exodus-Deuteronomy (four books into one chapter) to the more ample space afforded to 1 Samuel (one book reflected in four chapters).

Then—starting again as it were, but from a higher point—there is another progression from the relative reduction imposed on 2 Samuel (one book in one chapter) to the very ample space given to the second half of 2 Kings (half a book in five chapters).

This half book (2 Kings 14–25) is just twelve chapters, thus giving a situation whereby the subject-matter of these chapters—the fall of both Israel and Judah—receives huge attention. The overall impression then is of a mirror which does indeed reflect those at the back of a long room, but a mirror in which those who stand closer loom much larger.

A somewhat similar phenomenon occurs in Chronicles. But Chronicles' history is even more disproportionate: everything before David is reduced to two chapters (1 Chronicles 1–2).

INTERIM CONCLUSION

The events of the Elijah-Elisha narrative, despite their uniqueness, have central affinities with many of the most striking events in each of the great sections of the Primary History. The main lines of these affinities occur in the same order.

The remarkable similarities are matched by the basic intelligibility of the huge differences. These difference are not hodge-podge. Again and again, while echoing the Primary History, they switch the emphasis from figures of external power to figures of prophecy. The process therefore is coherent. The story of Genesis-Kings, instead of being regarded primarily as a record of history, has been mirrored above all as a bearer of God's word.

The conclusion which accounts for the data is not complicated: a prophetic writer, having been inspired in some way by the figures of Elijah and Elisha, used them as a filter to synthesize and interpret the Primary History.

To solidify this conclusion it is necessary to examine the texts in somewhat greater detail.

CHAPTER 3

A SYNTHESIS OF
THE PRIMARY HISTORY:
A MORE DETAILED COMPARISON

Without attempting a full analysis, this chapter compares the texts more closely and indicates some of the detailed links between the Elijah-Elisha narrative and the rest of the Primary History.

In reflecting Genesis, the Elijah-Elisha narrative not only singles out one leading episode (the flood), it also uses that episode as a kind of framework or foundation for reflecting other Genesis material. Likewise with other books or blocks: one episode or section generally provides an initial framework.

At first these framework texts are generally taken from near the beginning of the book in question (the flood, for instance, from near the beginning of Genesis), but as the Elijah-Elisha narrative goes on it tends, occasionally, to take its framework text from a later part of the book or block.

In comparison with the rest of the Primary History, the Elijah-Elisha narrative diminishes the roles of various kinds of people, including women, kings, and priests. Chronicles restores the emphasis on priests.

The Elijah-Elisha narrative not only reflects the various books, it also adapts them to the purpose and shape of its own narrative. As already emphasized, the Elijah-Elisha episodes involve two kinds of relationships—internal and external. In particular, the Primary History has to be mirrored in a way that maintains diptych structure. The second series of texts about the Aramean wars

(2 Kings 6–8), for instance, in addition to reflecting the warlike schismatic situation in the Primary History (1 Kings 12–16), also constructs its own diptych and maintains basic narrative continuity with the earlier account of Aramean wars (1 Kings 20).

The following comparison builds on the accompanying outline (Table 3.1). Where the matter is clear, the outline sometimes uses italics to highlight the foundational links between the texts. Thus, in the Genesis section, the flood is highlighted. Question marks indicate uncertainty.

TABLE 3.1:
THE MIRRORING OF GENESIS-KINGS IN ELIJAH-ELISHA: ASPECTS OF MORE DETAILS

GENESIS (THE FLOOD)	1 KGS 16:29–18:46 (THE DROUGHT)
Creation: all-powerful commanding word	Water: all-powerful commanding word (17:1)
FLOOD: sin, Noah, rain; turnaround, sacrifice, rainbow	*DROUGHT: sin, Elijah, no rain; turnaround, sacrifice, cloud*
Abraham: call, promise, blessing, son	"Go . . .": promise of food; son fed, revived
Jacob and his twelve sons	Twelve stones: "sons of Jacob"
Joseph: viceroy, food, recognition	Obadiah: steward, food, recognition

EXODUS-DEUTERONOMY (MOSES)	1 KINGS 19 (HOREB)
MOSES AT HOREB: flight after killing; encounter with God (burning bush); meeting with Aaron	*ELIJAH AT HOREB: flight after killings; encounter with God; meeting with Elisha*
Plagues; sea crossing (control of nature)	?? [Fire consumes water (ch. 18)]
The wilderness: food supplied, 40 years	The wilderness: food supplied, 40 days
Theophany at Sinai	Theophany at Horeb
Leviticus: true worship	?? [False worship condemned (16:29-34)]

(Table 3.1 cont.)

Numbers: the twelve tribes . . .	?? [12 stones; 12 tribes . . . of Jacob (18:31)]
Deuteronomy: Moses, the unique prophet	Elijah, the only surviving prophet
The appointment of a successor, Joshua	The call of a successor, Elisha

JOSHUA (WAR OF CONQUEST)	1 KINGS 20 (WAR AGAINST CONQUEST)
Joshua sends spies to Jericho	Aram sends messengers to Samaria
Crossing the Jordan	[Elijah/Elisha cross the Jordan (2 Kgs 2:7-14)]
SIEGE OF JERICHO, AI: approach city; powerful defenders; priests; direct attack; walls fall; victory; ban defied; punishment; second attack (Ai); victory	*SIEGE OF SAMARIA, APHEK: approach city; powerful attackers; prophet; direct attack; victory; second attack (Aphek); victory; walls fall; ban defied; punishment*
Israel with God on Mount Ebal (8:30-35)	Israel's god: a god of the mountains (20:23)
Gibeonites' treaty by trickery (ch. 9)	Aram's treaty by trickery (20:31-34)

JUDGES (KILLING, NO KING IN ISRAEL)	1 KINGS 21 (NABOTH; JEZEBEL REPLACES KING)
Achsah asks for a field (1:14)	Request for Naboth's field
Deborah takes over; Jael kills	*Jezebel takes over, to kill*
Woman kills with a millstone (9:52-54)	Naboth stoned to death
Messengers: avenge killing (19:30)	Messages: set up a killing

1 SAMUEL (PROPHET/WARS)	1 KINGS 22–2 KINGS 3 (PROPHETS/WARS)
Prophetic Samuel; Saul dies in battle (chs. 1–15, 31, esp. ch. 3)	Prophetic Micaiah and Ahab's death in battle (1 Kings 22) [Two formulaic reigns, 22:41-54]
Goliath: rejected/doomed Saul sends three groups to get David (chs. 16–18)	Doomed Ahaziah sends three groups of soldiers to get Elijah (2 Kings 1)

(Table 3.1 cont.)

David, Jonathan: companions against death (chs. 19–21, esp. ch. 20)	Elijah and Elisha walk through death (2 Kings 2)
David: wars/wanderings in the wilderness (chs. 22–30)	The Moabite war in the wilderness (2 Kings 3)

2 SAMUEL (DAVID)	2 KINGS 4 (POWER, WAR, WOMEN)
David takes over his kingship (chs. 1–10)	?? [Elisha takes over (2 Kgs 2:19-25)]
[Nathan's illustrative story (12:1-7)]	Illustrative story (4:1-7)
BATHSHEBA: man on roof; bed; conception	*SHUNAMMITESS: roof, bed (4:8-37)*
Messages (king and commander, ch. 11)	Message for king/commander? Conceives
The son's head (Absalom), death (chs. 14, 18–19)	The son's head, death
Running to tell of the son's death	Hurrying to tell of the son's death
A second runner . . . seeing the runner coming	Seeing her hurrying; running to meet her
First runner does not tell of death	Woman does not tell the runner
Second runner tells implicitly: son is dead	Woman tells implicitly: son is dead
David mourns the son	Elisha raises the son
Famine: death at barley harvest (ch. 21)	Famine: deathly soup; meal; no more death; barley loaves beat counting (4:38-44)
Census: famine? harvest; plague ends (ch. 24)	

1 KINGS 1–11 (SOLOMON'S GLORY)	2 KINGS 5 (NAAMAN'S GOLD)
Solomon as king, sage, builder (chs. 1–9)	??
QUEEN OF SHEBA: foreign dignitary; rich; comes to test Israel's king	*NAAMAN: foreign dignitary; rich; seeks a cure in Israel*

(Table 3.1 cont.)

Acknowledges Israel's God; gives gold	Accepts Israel's God; gold refused
Solomon's money and chariots	Gehazi, at chariot, seeks money
Solomon swayed by his foreign wives	?? [Naaman guided by little Israelite girl]

1 KINGS 12–16 (SCHISM, PROPHET)	2 KINGS 6–8 (WAR, PROPHET)
Schism: Rehoboam's war-bent army sent home by a man of God (ch. 12)	War: Elisha captures Aram's army and sends them home
PROPHETIC power/truth (ch. 13)	*PROPHETIC power/truth: siege (chs. 6–7)*
The wife of Jeroboam comes to the prophet about her sick son; the prophet announces punishment; the child dies (ch. 14)	The woman whose son Elisha raised to life is further cared for; sick Ben-haded consults Elisha and dies (8:1-15)
Eight formulaic reigns (14:21–16:28)	Two formulaic reigns (8:16-29)
Elijah-Elisha (1 Kgs 16:29– 2 Kgs 13:25)	

2 KINGS 14–17 (ISRAEL'S MURDEROUS END)	2 KINGS 9–10 (JEHU)
Israel: murderous reigns and final fall—because of idolatry/Baal, and despite prophetic warnings	Jehu's murders and destruction of Israel's house—because of Baal, and with prophetic instigation

2 KINGS 18–25 (REFORM; FALL)	2 KINGS 11–13 (REFORM; DEATH)
*Hezekiah: deathly illness, recovery (20)	
Murderous Manasseh (21)	Murderous Athaliah (11:1)
YOUNG JOSIAH: law discovered in Temple leads to initiation of reform (chs. 22–23)	*YOUNG JOASH: hidden in the Temple, emerges to initiate reform (chs. 11–12)*
Formulaic reigns (23:31–24:20)	Formulaic reigns (13:1-13)

(Table 3.1 cont.)

	*Elisha: deathly illness; miracle (13:14-21)
Deathly Babylonian invasion; fall (25:1-26)	Death and a Moabite incursion (see 13:20)
The king: restoration hinted (25:27–30)	The cities: restoration is clear . . . because of Abraham/Isaac/Jacob (13:22-25)

THE MORE DETAILED COMPARISON

THE DROUGHT (1 KGS 16:29–18:46): A VARIATION ON GENESIS, ESPECIALLY ON THE FLOOD (GEN 6:1–9:17)

To reflect Genesis, the later narrative takes what is probably Genesis' most dramatic story, the flood, turns it over to become the story of a great drought, and then uses that drought story as the setting or framework for other reflections of Genesis.

Use of Genesis therefore is of two basic kinds: use of the foundational flood story and use of the rest of the book.

USE OF THE FLOOD STORY

Some of the shared elements are as follows:

The introduction: an evil situation leads to crisis. Genesis (6:1-8) tells of wayward marriages and the spread of evil (the sons of God marry the daughters of men), and 1 Kings (16:29-34) recounts Ahab's evil, compounded by his marriage (Ahab marries Jezebel). In both cases the marriages distort true relationship to God; the true sense of God is lost. The Genesis marriages confuse God with humans. Marriage to Jezebel replaces God with Baal. While the confusion in Genesis is of a mythical kind, the confusion in 1 Kings is limited to the proportions of history. In other words, it is adapted to the genre of the book.

The introduction continued: evil is compounded (Gen 6:4; 1 Kgs 16:34). Having given the basic picture of idolatrous marriage, both texts then recount a complication involving children. "In those days" the distorted marriages of Genesis gave birth to children (6:4). And "in those days" Hiel of Bethel rebuilt Jericho at the cost of his children (1 Kgs 16:34). One may argue as to which are the more monstrous, the births or the deaths, but both are terribly awry. Again, however, while the Genesis account is largely mythical, that of 1 Kings is adapted to the dimensions of history. The picture in 1 Kings is also adapted to the subsequent narrative: the killing of the sons sets the scene for the later saving of sons/children by Elijah and Elisha (1 Kings 17; 2 Kings 4).

Suddenly, a true servant of YHWH: Noah, Elisha. To save them from the flood/drought, God gives the servant challenging instructions—to go into an ark/wadi until eventually everything is flooded/dried up (Gen 6:9–7:24; 1 Kgs 17:1-7).

Later, a dramatic change by God: stopping the rain for Noah and telling Elisha of rain to come (Gen 8:1-14; 1 Kgs 18:1-2).

In the presence of all creatures/Israel, Noah and Elijah (re)build an altar and offer burnt offerings (Gen 8:15-22; 1 Kgs 18:30, 38). Curiously, while Genesis then gives the command not to kill (Gen 9:1-6), Elijah kills the prophets of Baal (1 Kgs 18:40; this killing is hardly to be regarded as praiseworthy; see Chapter 1, n. 18).

Finally, the sign for the end of the flood/drought: the rainbow (Gen 9:8-17) and the cloud (1 Kgs 18:41-46). The flood story ends with the sign of a rainbow, which is set in the clouds ("clouds" occurs four times, combined with references to water, a flood, and God's gathering of the clouds, Gen 9:14-16). The end of the drought on the other hand is signaled by repeated references to rain, sea, and cloud—beginning with a cloud as small as a man's hand and ending with clouds that darken the skies (1 Kgs 18:41-45). The essence of both texts is that the rain-related signal (rainbow/cloud) indicates God's faithfulness: God promises, with a covenant, not to bring the flood again (Gen 9:12-17), and God fulfills the declaration, made earlier, that rain could come at his word (1 Kgs 17:1). (The Elijah-Elisha narrative does not use the concept of the covenant until the very end, 2 Kgs 13:23.) Genesis depicts God's promise being made; 1 Kings tells of God's promise being fulfilled.

TABLE 3.2:
THE MIRRORING OF GENESIS IN 1 KGS 16:29–18:37:
LEADING ASPECTS

GENESIS	1 KGS 16:29–18:46
Creation and creation-related flood (Genesis 1–11)	Drought and creation-like control over nature (16:29–17:6)
Abraham relying on God's word: a foreign journey involving a woman and a food crisis, and a God-given son (Genesis 12–25)	Elijah, relying on God's word, goes to a Sidonian town; a woman gives him food and God restores her son (17:7-24)
*** Jacob, man of conflict; father of Israel's twelve sons/tribes (Genesis 25–36)	++ Obadiah ("servant of YHWH"), master of the palace, provider of food, devout since youth (18:1-19)
++ Joseph, youthful dreamer, faithful servant, master of Pharaoh's realm, provider of food (Genesis 37–50)	*** Conflict on Mount Carmel, gathering all Israel, and recalling Jacob's twelve tribes/sons (18:20-40)

USE OF THE REST OF GENESIS

Within the framework of the drought account there are reflections of other aspects of Genesis. As partly indicated in the accompanying outline (Table 3.2), some of these aspects are as follows:

God's word—the commanding word at creation (Genesis 1)—is reflected in God's commanding of the elements at the beginning of the drought. Even the verbal pattern of 1 Kgs 17:1-6, described by several researchers as one of "command and compliance,"[1] fits well with the command-and-compliance pattern of Genesis 1.

Key aspects of *the story of Abraham* all find a variant echo in Elijah's departure for foreign Zarephath (1 Kgs 17:8-24). As Abraham once set out for a foreign land, relying on God's word, so does Elijah, in his own way. On reaching the foreign land there is

---

[1] See Jerome Walsh, "The Elijah Cycle: A Synchronic Approach" (Ph.D. diss., Univ. of Michigan, 1982) 22.

a crisis involving a woman and food: Sarah and famine in Egypt (Genesis 12), and the Sidonian widow and food (1 Kgs 17:10-11). Unlike Abraham and Sarah who, as a couple, fail in the crisis—fear of famine drives them to disturbing compromises—Elijah and the widow are radically faithful to God's word.

As the Abraham story becomes increasingly dominated by the desire for a child and by the history surrounding a child, so the story of Elijah and the widow begins to focus increasingly on her son. Isaac was a sheer gift of God—both in his birth and in his rescue from sacrificial death—and, in a very different way, the widow's son also becomes a gift of God, a life restored by prayer to YHWH (17:12-24).

Thus the essence of the Abraham story—radical reliance on God's life-giving word—is distilled into just eighteen verses (17:7-24). The distillation is hugely different and if 1 Kings 17 were taken in isolation the relationship to the Abraham story would seem questionable or coincidental. But when placed within the larger pattern of literary relationships—the larger mirroring of Genesis and the Primary History as a whole—it begins to become clear that the apparent coincidence is no accident. As for the differences between Elijah and Abraham, they become intelligible in light of the distinctive requirements of the later narrative. The story of Elijah and the Sidonian widow is not just refracting Abraham; it is also preparing the way for the rest of the Elijah-Elisha narrative—a text which, more than Genesis, places explicit emphasis on the word, especially on prophecy.

Jacob and his twelve sons are recalled briefly but explicitly as Elijah is about to offer sacrifice (18:31). It seems difficult to say, pending further research, whether the fiercely conflictive nature of the confrontation on Mount Carmel reflects anything of the conflictive nature of Jacob's life—his struggles with Esau and Laban, especially his confrontation with Laban and his idols on Mount Gilead (Gen 31:11-54).

The story of Joseph, the viceroy who kept Israel's family alive, is reflected in the account of Ahab's steward Obadiah, who provided food for the prophets of YHWH and who recognized Elijah (1 Kgs 18:3-15, esp. 18:3-4, 7). Like Joseph, Obadiah has a double allegiance, to the monarch and to YHWH, and, also like Joseph, there is reference to his youth (1 Kgs 18:12).

Elijah's final prayer (1 Kgs 18:36) is to the God of "Abraham, Isaac and Jacob"—three names that to some degree summarize Genesis and that are so used in Genesis' final scene (Gen 50:24).

Though many details have not been clarified, the basic conclusion is straightforward: the author of the beginning of the Elijah story (1 Kgs 16:29–18:46) had the essential Genesis text and, while writing a new account—Elijah is distinctive—synthesized and adapted many of Genesis' basic aspects.

FLIGHT TO HOREB, A CALL, AND A HELPER
(MOSES, ESPECIALLY MOSES' CALL,
EXOD 2:13–4:31; 1 KINGS 19)

In dealing with the long life of Moses (Exodus-Deuteronomy), the interpretive narrative again chooses an early defining moment and uses it as a framework. This defining framework—a combination of Moses' flight to the desert (after killing an Egyptian) and his subsequent encounter with God at Horeb/Sinai (Exod 2:13–4:31)—provides a framework for Elijah's flight (after killing the prophets of Baal) and for his later encounter with God at Horeb (1 Kings 19).

When the encounter is over, both Moses and Elijah return from Horeb and meet a helper, respectively Aaron (Exod 4:13-31) and Elisha (1 Kgs 19:15-19).

Into this Horeb framework the later narrative (1 Kings 19) distills various other elements of the life of Moses: the thunderous meeting at the mountain, the supplying of food in the wilderness, the journey for forty years/days, and the appointment of a successor (Joshua/Elisha). Continuity with Moses is strong: "it is clear that Elijah was a religious leader of the calibre . . . of Moses. . . . His career echoed that of Moses in a number of important ways. . . . The legends of Elisha's miracles were selected to illustrate certain Mosaic features in that prophet's work."[2] This comment involves a historical claim which is debatable, but its basic point is valid: in the biblical text, Elijah echoes Moses.

---

[2] Robert Carroll, "The Elijah-Elisha Sagas: Some Remarks on Prophetic Succession in Ancient Israel," *VT* 19 (1969) 412–13.

The relationship is not only to Exodus. Donald Wiseman,[3] for instance, connects the Horeb scene with Deuteronomy also:

> The *forty days and forty nights* marks a long time and identifies Elijah as a second Moses (Ex. 24:18; 34:28; Dt. 9:8-10). . . . The upheaval of nature [at Horeb] is reminiscent of the covenant at Sinai and the commissioning of Moses and the people (Ex. 19:9,16; 34:6; Dt. 5:23-26). . . . Elijah realized that he, like Moses, could not look at God's face and live (cf. Ex 33:20-22; cf. Gn. 32:30) so he covered his face.

Two important elements of Moses' life—the negative confrontation with Pharaoh and the positive imparting of revelation and worship at Sinai—may have contributed as components to the earlier scene on Carmel (the negative confrontation with the Baalites and the positive revelation and sacrifice, 1 Kgs 18:20-39). Thus while the main lines of the Elijah-Elisha narrative follow precisely the order of the main line of the Primary History, individual elements are sometimes rearranged.

Further features may, perhaps, be connected:

(1) The importance of true worship: The central importance of worship, stated positively at the center of Exodus-Deuteronomy, is stated negatively at the beginning of the Elijah narrative in the picture of Ahab, especially in the portrayal of idolatrous Jezebel and of Hiel's infanticide (1 Kgs 16:29-34).

(2) Control over nature: God shows control over plagues in Egypt, and over water and fire on Mount Carmel.

(3) The prophet as unique yet replaceable: Moses was unique (Deut 34:10-12) yet Joshua received some of his spirit (Deut 34:9) and God promised to raise up someone like him (Deut 18:15-18). And Elijah, despite his own kind of uniqueness (1 Kgs 19:10, 14), is to be replaced by Elisha (1 Kgs 19:16).

Here, even more than in the use of Genesis, there is an opening for prolonged analysis, analysis which concentrates first of all on the finished texts (on 1 Kings 19 and Exodus-Deuteronomy).

---

[3] Donald J. Wiseman, *1 and 2 Kings,* Tyndale OT Commentaries (Leicester: Inter-Varsity, 1993) 172–3.

However, while the details need further work, the basic conclusion is clear: the portrayal of Elijah at Horeb (1 Kings 19) mirrors several features of the life of Moses (Exodus-Deuteronomy).

INVADING/INVADED: THE WAR FOR/AGAINST CONQUEST (JOSHUA; 1 KINGS 20)

Following the story of Moses, the next book to be reflected is Joshua with its war of conquest. The Elijah-Elisha narrative keeps the basic idea of conquest but, as with the flood-drought relationship, turns it around: the war of conquest (Joshua) becomes a war against conquest (by Aram, 1 Kings 20). The challenge of taking the land has been turned into the challenge of keeping the land.

In dealing with the book of Joshua, the later narrative again singles out an early dramatic moment—the siege of Jericho and Ai (Josh 5:13–8:29). This double siege (Jericho/Ai) provides the framework for Aram's double siege, namely against Samaria and Aphek. Aspects of the framework:

- the army approaches the city (Josh 2; 5:13; 1 Kgs 20:1);
- the attackers send spies (Joshua 2) or messengers (1 Kgs 20:2-11);
- apparently the city has strong defense/attackers (Josh 6:1; 1 Kgs 20:10);
- a non-military intervention (priests, Josh 6:4-16; a prophet, 1 Kgs 20:13-14);
- a sudden direct attack into/out of the city (Josh 6:20; 1 Kgs 20:15-17);
- a total/great victory (Josh 6:21; 1 Kgs 20:20-21);
- the second attack, on Ai/Aphek (Joshua 7; 1 Kgs 20:26-27);
- another victory (Joshua 8; 1 Kgs 20:28-30).

Within this framework of sieges (1 Kings 20) there are other aspects of the book of Joshua:

- walls fall down (Josh 6:20; 1 Kgs 20:30);
- a ban is defied and the defiance punished (Joshua 7; 1 Kgs 20:34, 42);

- Israel's God is a God of the mountains (Ebal; Josh 8:30-35; 1 Kgs 20:23).

A more detailed example comes from the unique story of the Gibeonites.

Israel's treaty with the Gibeonites (Joshua 9) is distilled to provide one component for the account of Ahab's treaty with Ben-haded (1 Kgs 20:31-34). In both cases a weak(ened) enemy (the Gibeonites/Ben-haded) who "has heard" of Israel's history or nature (Josh 9:9; 1 Kgs 20:31) decides to put on an appearance of road-weariness or repentance (the Gibeonites have old sacks and worn clothing; Ben-haded's servants wear sackcloth and ropes). Thus attired, they approach the victorious Israelites. Their essential purpose in both cases is that their lives be spared; to ensure this they ask for a treaty (Josh 9:11, 15; 1 Kgs 20:32, 34). The Israelites are deceived by appearances: Joshua's forces make a treaty with the Gibeonites (Josh 9:15) and Ahab makes a treaty with Ben-haded (1 Kgs 20:34). Afterward, however, there is regret: the people complain to the leaders (Josh 9:18) and a member of the prophetic brotherhoods reprimands Ahab (1 Kgs 20:39-43).

Further aspects of the book of Joshua appear to be reflected either in 1 Kings 20 or elsewhere. For instance, the crossing of the Jordan (Joshua 3–4) is echoed in the crossing of the Jordan by Elijah and Elisha (2 Kgs 2:8, 14-15).

Overall, in this case (the Aramean invasion, 1 Kings 20) the dependence on a section of the Primary History (on the book of Joshua) is unusually clear. The similarity is not only in the sudden centrality of war but in many of the war's details.

THE WOMEN/WOMAN AND THE KILLING OF THE INNOCENT (JUDGES; 1 KINGS 21, NABOTH)

Having distilled Joshua's conquest (the book of Joshua), adapting it to the time of Elijah and Ahab, the Elijah-Elisha narrative then turns its attention to the book of Judges.

The terrible events in the book of Judges, particularly the killings, take place when there is no king in Israel (Judg 18:1; 19:1; 21:25), and so the next event in the Elijah-Elisha narrative, the killing of Naboth, occurs when in effect there is no king in

Israel—because Jezebel takes over the kingship. She mocks the king because he cannot get the field he wants and then she takes charge (1 Kgs 21:7).

The particular part of Judges which provides the basic framework for the killing of Naboth (1 Kings 21) is Judges 4, the narrative leading up to the killing of Sisera: first a woman takes over the leadership of Israel from a man (Deborah from Barak; Jezebel from Ahab) and then a woman kills a man (Jael kills Sisera directly; Jezebel kills Naboth indirectly). The roles of both Deborah and Jael have been fused into that of Jezebel: she takes the leadership and she kills.

The rest of the book of Judges—particularly the leading role played by a sequence of women—helps to fill out this basic framework of the Naboth story:

- a woman (Achsah) demands a field (Judg 1:14) and Ahab demands Naboth's field (1 Kgs 21:1-3);
- a woman in effect kills Abimelech by stoning (with a millstone, Judg 9:52-54), and Naboth is stoned indirectly by a woman, Jezebel (1 Kgs 21:14);
- a woman is killed and messengers are sent around (Judg 19:29), and Jezebel sends messages for a killing (1 Kgs 21:8-9). In other words, the stark Judges picture of sending messages—the parts of a dead woman are used as messages to summon the people to come together to deliver justice— is turned around to depict a woman who, under pretense of seeking to deliver justice, summons the people so that she can have someone killed.

The Naboth account involves a synthesis of two basic threads in Judges. Many of the women-related episodes of Judges have been synthesized around the figure of Jezebel. And the suffering endured in Judges has been synthesized around Naboth.

This synthesis involves a strong element of interpretation. Not all the women in Judges are harmless and honorable, yet by and large, beginning with energetic Achsah (Judg 1:14), they emerge primarily as either strong or suffering. However, Jezebel, the woman character in the Elijah story, is indeed strong but she is not suffering. The suffering, curiously, has been portrayed through a man, Naboth.

PROPHETS, WARRIORS, COMPANIONS, AND WAR IN THE WILDERNESS
(1 SAMUEL; 1 KINGS 22–2 KINGS 3)

As noted in discussing quantity analysis, the later events/books of the Primary History receive relatively more space in the Elijah-Elisha narrative. So it is that the thirty-one chapters of 1 Samuel occupy all of four chapters (1 Kings 22–2 Kings 3).

1 Samuel may be divided into roughly four sections: (1) 1–15: Prophet Samuel and Saul (plus Saul's death in battle, ch. 31); (2) 16–19: David, mighty fighter, pursued by Saul; (3) 20–21: David and Jonathan (companions); (4) 22–30: David's warlike wanderings in the wilderness.

These four sections appear to be reflected obliquely in four successive chapters of the Elijah-Elisha narrative (1 Kings 22–2 Kings 3). At times the reflection is reasonably clear, but at other times, particularly concerning David's overpowering of Goliath, it is elusive. In oversimplified terms, the continuity between the texts is outlined in Table 3.3.

Taking the four sections of Table 3.3 singly some further connections begin to emerge:

THE PROPHET AND THE KING'S DEATH IN BATTLE
(1 SAMUEL 1–15; 31; 1 KINGS 22)

In the account of Ahab's death (1 Kings 22) the primary emphasis is not on military strategy but on the difficult search beforehand for a true prophet of YHWH, someone not afraid to say what is going to happen. Eventually they find a true prophet, Micaiah, who eventually tells of coming disaster (1 Kgs 22:6-9, 13-17).

The minimal framework for describing the difficult call of Micaiah apparently comes from the call of Samuel (1 Samuel 3). As the call of Samuel was difficult—it had to be repeated three times before Samuel heard God's truth (1 Sam 3:4, 6, 8-10)—so in effect the question to the prophets has to be repeated three times before eventually Micaiah speaks God's truth (1 Kgs 22:6, 15, 17). And that truth is difficult enough to make both Samuel and Micaiah hesitate before pronouncing it: Samuel announced to Eli the condemnation of his house (1 Sam 3:11-14, 18), and Micaiah in effect announced to Ahab his impending death (1 Kgs 22:17).

TABLE 3.3:
THE MIRRORING OF 1 SAMUEL IN 1 KINGS 22–2 KINGS 3:
LEADING ASPECTS

1 SAMUEL	1 KINGS 22–2 KINGS 3
Prophetic Samuel; Saul's death in battle (chs. 1–15 and 31).	Prophetic Micaiah; Ahab's death in battle (1 Kings 22).
Defeat of Goliath (chs 16–18). Saul, rejected/doomed, sends three groups to capture David; they are overcome by prophetic spirit (ch. 19).	———— Ahaziah, fallen, doomed, rejected, sends three groups of soldiers to capture Elijah; they are killed/overawed by prophetic fire (2 Kings 1).
[Gen 5:24: God takes Enoch.] [Joshua 3–5: Crossing the Jordan.] David, Jonathan: companions against death (ch. 21).	YHWH will take Elijah. Crossing the Jordan. Elijah and Elisha walk together toward death (2 Kings 2).
David: wars/wanderings in the wilderness (chs. 22–30).	The Moabite war in the wilderness (2 Kings 3).

Around this prophecy-centered framework 1 Kings has filtered various elements from 1 Samuel 1–15, among them:

- Horsey monarchies: what is warned against at the monarchy's foundation (1 Samuel 8) is seen in Ahab and Jehoshaphat (1 Kgs 22:1-3, 8).
- War-scenes: in place of the defense of Jabesh-gilead (1 Samuel 11), there is a plan to attack Ramoth-gilead (1 Kgs 22:3).
- A prophet-king clash: the Samuel-Saul confrontation (1 Samuel 12–15, especially chs. 13 and 15) provides part of the dynamic for the tension between Micaiah and Ahab (1 Kgs 22:15-28). Like Samuel, Micaiah confronts the king at a sensitive time—in the context of facing battle (1 Sam 13:8-15; 1 Kgs 22:13-16). In particular, Micaiah's image of

Ahab's army as scattered sheep (1 Kgs 22:17) seems to combine diverse images from Saul's campaign—the initial dispersing or scattering of his army (1 Sam 13:11), and the subsequent crisis about the sheep ("What is this bleating of sheep?" 1 Sam 15:14). In both confrontations the king is condemned, and then there is an indication of the king's approaching death. In Saul's case the death is merely intimated—through the death of another king, Agag (1 Samuel 32–35). In the case of Ahab, the coming death is implied more clearly: Micaiah stakes his credibility as a prophet on a claim that the king will not return safe from the battle (1 Kgs 22:28).

The lying spirit from God, tricking Ahab (1 Kgs 22:20-22), may reflect a later part of 1 Samuel—the evil spirit from God, which disturbs Saul (1 Sam 19:8-10).

In the battle (1 Samuel 31; 1 Kgs 22:29-38) there are a number of continuities and variations:

- Each king is hit, unluckily, by an arrow: Saul is caught off guard, Ahab is struck by a random shot.
- The arrows do not kill them, and both make a request: Saul says, "Kill me"; Ahab says, "Get me out."
- The requests are not met: Saul's armor-bearer is unwilling and Ahab's charioteer is unable.
- The king dies in battle: Saul on his own sword, Ahab in his chariot.

Both accounts go on to tell of the flight of the Israelites and the burial of the king. The tone surrounding the two burials is very different (1 Sam 32:7-13; 1 Kgs 31:36-38).

OVERCOMING WARRIORS: DAVID HUNTED BY SAUL (1 SAMUEL 16–19) AND ELIJAH HUNTED BY AHAZIAH (2 KINGS 1)

The opening chapter of 2 Kings has a strong contrast: a fallen king who lies on his sick bed and an endangered prophet who sits on a hill and calls down fire from heaven. The sick king, Ahaziah, sends messengers to consult Baalzebub, but the prophet, Elijah, intercepts them in the name of God. It is after this interception that Elijah, found on a mountain, backs his declaration of God with heavenly fire.

This account is unusually difficult, at least as concerns its relationship to the preceding Primary History. It seems likely, in view of the larger pattern, that some element of David's victory over Goliath is reflected in the account of how the lone Elijah, sitting on the mountain, used the fire from heaven to overcome the three contingents of fifty soldiers who came to capture him (2 Kgs 1:9-16). More obviously than in the David scene, credit for the victory goes to the God of Israel.

However, even if the Goliath drama has some influence on 2 Kings 1, that influence is very limited. This chapter involves not just one factor but several.

Among these other possible factors, the following may be noted:

- As indicated earlier (in analyzing the diptych structure, Chapter 2), 2 Kings 1 is shaped to complement the pivotal account of Elijah's fiery ascent to heaven (2 Kings 2).
- The doomed king, Ahaziah, corresponds partly to Saul, the king who has been rejected by the prophet and whose death has been intimated (1 Sam 15:23, 32-35).
- Ahaziah's sending of three contingents to capture the prophet Elijah on the mountain (2 Kgs 1:9-15) corresponds significantly to Saul's sending of three groups to capture David on the prophetic hill/mountain of Ramah (1 Sam 19:18-21). In both cases the three groups are overcome by a prophetic spirit (1 Sam 19:20-21) or by a prophetic fire (2 Kgs 1:9-15).
- Several descriptions of appearance or clothing—victorious David's countenance (1 Sam 16:12; 17:42), Michal's goat-haired dummy of David (1 Sam 19:13), Saul's prophetic loss of clothing (1 Sam 19:24)—have contributed variously toward the unusual process of describing Elijah's clothing (2 Kgs 1:8).

It is useful to list some of the shared elements (see Table 3.4).

TABLE 3.4:
ESCAPING THE KING:
ASPECTS OF 1 SAM 19:8-24 MIRRORED IN 2 KINGS 1

1 SAM 19:8-24	2 KINGS 1
War! (David vs. Philistines)	Rebellion! (Moab vs. Israel)
Saul sends messengers to kill David.	The king sends messengers.
Michal: Escape or you will be dead.	You will surely die.
From a window, she lets David down.	Fall from upper lattice/balcony.
Michal lays teraphim/oracle . . .	Consulting the god.
. . . on a bed,	The bed you are in.
goat hair at the head,	Wearing a garment of haircloth,
and covered with clothing.	with a leather loincloth.
Michal to messengers: He is ill.	He lay ill.
Saul sends messengers again:	Messengers come back.
Bring him to me in the bed,	You will not get out of bed;
so I may kill him.	you will die.
David flees to Samuel at Ramah.	———
Saul sends messengers	Ahaziah sends fifty soldiers
to capture David;	to make Elijah come.
but seeing the prophets prophesying,	———
with Samuel over them,	
the Spirit of God	Fire comes from heaven
came upon the messengers of Saul,	and destroys the soldiers.
and they also prophesied.	———
Saul sends other messengers.	Ahaziah sends fifty more
and they too prophesied.	and fire destroys them also.
Saul sends a third group,	Ahaziah sends a third group
and they also prophesied.	and they ask to escape the fire.
Saul in Ramah on a hilltop (?).	Elijah on a hill/mountain.

Details are debatable, including Saul's location on a hilltop
(1 Sam 19:22; the text is obscure), but the overall correspondence
is noteworthy.

COMPANIONS IN THE FACE OF DEATH: DAVID AND JONATHAN
(1 SAMUEL 19–21), ELIJAH AND ELISHA (2 KINGS 2)

Elijah's crossing of the Jordan and ascent to heaven (2 Kings 2) seems to involve a synthesizing of very diverse factors. This dense synthesizing probably reflects the pivotal nature of the diptych, especially of the ascent (2 Kings 2).

Two reflections of the earlier Primary History are easy to detect: God's taking of Elijah announced at the very beginning of the chapter (2 Kgs 2:1) develops the Genesis reference to God's taking of Enoch (Gen 5:24). And Elijah's dry-shod crossing of the Jordan (2 Kgs 2:8) distills the longer account of Joshua's similar crossing (Joshua 3–5).

But the account of Elijah's ascent also keeps pace with developments in 1 Samuel. Elisha's fidelity to Elijah, walking with him into the face of death, involves a refraction of the fierce fidelity between David and Jonathan—even in face of death (1 Samuel 20). Here, as in other Elijah-Elisha texts, there is a shift toward prophecy and prophets. The military aspect of the David and Jonathan story—including the enigmatic shooting of arrows (1 Samuel 20) and the taking of Goliath's sword (1 Samuel 21)—is not altogether omitted; rather, it contributes as one component to the picture of the fiery chariot and horses (2 Kings 2). The full background to the fiery chariot is probably quite complex.

WARLIKE WANDERINGS IN THE WILDERNESS
(1 SAMUEL 22–30; 2 KINGS 3)

The strange wandering war against Moab (2 Kings 3) reflects various aspects of David's wanderings in the wilderness (1 Samuel 22–30). Both accounts begin with diverse references to the king of Moab (1 Sam 22:3-4; 2 Kgs 3:4-5). Other shared elements include thousands and thousands of sheep (1 Sam 25:2; 2 Kgs 3:4), the need for provisions in the wilderness (1 Sam 22:10; 23:1, 5, 14; 2 Kings 3:9), and consultation about fighting (1 Sam 23:2-4; 2 Kgs 3:11).

Overall this section, with the use of 1 Samuel at the center of the Elijah-Elisha narrative (1 Kings 22–2 Kings 3), is so complex and difficult that in itself it could be the subject of a specialized study. Yet it is better at this stage, rather than engage the web of details, to try to keep a clear sense of the wider context—the general correspondence of the Elijah-Elisha story to the flow of the Primary History, and the broad tendency to shift from history to prophecy, especially from military exploits to events that are more clearly centered on God's word. The bond between Elijah and Elisha, for instance, may at first seem to have no relationship to the friendship of David and Jonathan, but, given the larger interpretive moves, the relationship is worth investigating.

Domestic Drama: The Women, the Children, and the News of Death (2 Samuel; 2 Kings 4)

Having allowed the reflection of a single book (1 Samuel) to occupy all of four chapters (1 Kings 22–2 Kings 3), the author of the Elijah-Elisha narrative starts over as it were by a partial return to the initial degree of compression: the reflection of 2 Samuel is distilled into a single chapter (2 Kings 4).

In synthesizing 2 Samuel the Elijah-Elisha narrative makes particular use of the accounts of Bathsheba and Absalom (2 Samuel 11–19). Instead of a king who, having seen a married woman from his roof, invites her to visit and conceives a child with her (2 Samuel 11), there is a prophet who, having been invited by a married woman to visit, in a room on the roof, conceives a child with her—implicitly by God's word (2 Kgs 4:8-17). Bathsheba is partly reflected—inversely—in the woman of Shunem.

But the child who is thus conceived dies. Bathsheba's child is struck by God, becomes seriously ill, and, despite David's prayers, dies on the seventh day (2 Sam 12:15-18). And the Shunammitess's child, after it grows up, also becomes ill and dies.

The manner of death, however, is very diverse. The author of the Elijah-Elisha narrative has blended the death accounts of two of David's children—Bathsheba's child and Absalom. Thus, instead of a son who has a fatal head injury—Absalom's head catches in a tree (2 Sam 14:24; 18:9-15)—and the announcement of whose death leads to an elaborate double process of running and greeting, of not revealing and revealing to the father (2 Sam 18:19-32), there is a son whose head illness leads to death (2 Kgs 4:18-20). The announcement of his death then leads his mother, the woman of Shunem, to an elaborate double process of hurrying and greeting, of not revealing and revealing (2 Kgs 4:21-37). In other words, the anguished drama of the mother who hurries past the running Gehazi in order to throw herself at the prophet's feet and implicitly announce the death of her son (2 Kgs 4:22-28) is a prophet-oriented variation on the dramatic account of the messengers who ran, one overtaking the other, to announce implicitly to David that his son was dead (2 Sam 18:19-32).

Again there is a great difference. When the death of the son is revealed all David can do is weep. But, because of the prophet, the mother receives her son back.

Other parts of 2 Kings 4 reflect other aspects of 2 Samuel, such as the story of the widow's oil (2 Kgs 4:1-7). The story of how Elisha helped the weakest (the widow about to lose her children) functions like the story of hurting the weakest (Nathan's parable about taking the childlike lamb, 2 Sam 12:1-15): it clarifies the character of the protagonist (David, Elisha) and acts as an adjunct to the larger story of a woman conceiving. Thus while the plots of these two stories—the oil and the lamb—are hugely diverse, they share significant similarity of function.

Another example is the poisoned soup (2 Kgs 4:38-41) and the multiplication of loaves (2 Kgs 4:42-44). These two episodes, dealing especially with famine, death, and a providence that defies counting, distill the complex episodes of 2 Samuel 21–24 (esp. chs. 21 and 24) concerning famine, death, and counting (census).

Thus all the episodes of 2 Kings 4—the women, soup, and bread—while having their own distinct identity and ethos, also reflect the complex history of David's household. The focus now, however, is not on the perils of the envious court but on the dangers and needs of daily life. The powerful court has been left behind and in its place is a new center of justice and strength—the prophetic word.

THE MEN OF GOLD: SOLOMON (1 KINGS 1–11) AND NAAMAN (2 KINGS 5)

Having reverted to a tight proportion of one book to one chapter (2 Samuel refracted into 2 Kings 4), the mirroring of the Primary History now begins, in spiraling manner, to become ample once again: the history of Solomon and the schism (1 Kings 1–16) is allotted four chapters (2 Kings 5–8). The initial part, the history of Solomon (1 Kings 1–11), receives one chapter (2 Kings 5). The adaptation is quite radical. Instead of Solomon, who, amid all his glory and gold, showed little interest in prophecy, the Elijah-Elisha narrative describes Naaman, a prestigious figure who, despite all his gold (his gift includes 6000 gold shekels [2 Kgs 5:5]), learns to listen to the prophet's word (2 Kgs 5:13-14).

The specific model which provides the literary framework for the Naaman story is the visit of the queen of Sheba (1 Kings 10). The basic similarities are easy to detect. In both cases a rich foreign dignitary, who is either royal or a royal official, comes to visit the leading person of Israel, the king or the prophet (Namaan gets it wrong at first; like the queen, he initially visits the king, 2 Kgs 5:6-7). The encounter with the leading figure proves immensely beneficial: the queen, having listened at length, blesses the God of Israel; and Naaman, with minimal verbal contact—the contrast is acute—eventually does likewise. Then, having additionally received the gift(s) they asked for from Israel's leading person, the visitors return home.

The question of gifts, in fact, involves another strong contrast. The queen of Sheba endowed Solomon with unparalleled presents (1 Kgs 9:10-11), and it is said that the whole world brought presents to Solomon in Israel (1 Kgs 10:24-25). But Elisha, Israel's prophet, accepted no present whatsoever (2 Kgs 5:15-16).

Both visits are followed by an emphasis on wealth and chariots: the account of Solomon's money and chariots (1 Kgs 10:14-29) and the story of Gehazi, who pursued Naaman's chariot for money (2 Kgs 5:20-27).

There is a further acute contrast between the women in the Solomon story, especially Solomon's wives, and a feminine figure in the Namaan story, the little Israelite girl who understood the role of the prophet (2 Kgs 5:2). The wives were as prestigious as could be imagined—seven hundred wives of royal rank, beginning with Pharaoh's daughter (1 Kgs 11:1-3). The Israelite girl, on the other hand, was a slave. The prestigious wives led Solomon's heart away from YHWH (1 Kgs 11:4-6), but the slave girl set Naaman on a path that eventually led to the worship of YHWH (2 Kgs 5:17-19).

Whatever the details, the basic pattern of interpretation remains. The Elijah-Elisha narrative not only distills and synthesizes the account of Solomon and the visit of the queen of Sheba, it also changes the essential focus from monarchy to prophecy. The story itself, concerning Naaman and Elisha, reflects the larger hermeneutical move: the leprous suppliant is told to go not to Israel's king but to its prophet (2 Kgs 5:5-8).

PROPHETS IN WAR: THE FULFILLMENT OF THE PROPHET'S WORD (1 KGS 12:1–16:28; 2 KINGS 6–8)

Following Solomon's death, the Primary History gives a long five-chapter account of the schism and of the emergence of two sets of monarchs, one in Judah, the other in (northern) Israel (1 Kgs 12:1–16:28). In 1 Kings 13, near the beginning of this long account, there is a striking story about a man of God who, having come to schismatic Bethel and demonstrated his powers, fails to persevere in adhering to the word of God; he leaves the word and gives priority to food. The result is disastrous: a lion kills him.

Aspects of this complex story about adhering to the word provided a basic framework for the equally complex stories concerning the role of Elisha during the later Aramean wars (2 Kings 6–7). The focus of the two sets of episodes (1 Kings 13; 2 Kings 6–7) is on prophetic insight, on seeing the truth and listening to the word.

At times the relationship between these texts is elusive. There are some curious similarities, for instance, between the prophetic condemnation of the Bethel altar (1 Kgs 13:1-10) and the prophet-backed project of building at the Jordan (2 Kgs 6:1-7). At the Bethel altar there is the brief but intense drama of the king who, in protest against the (destructive) prophetic sign, stretched out his hand against the man of God, only to find that the outstretched hand was withered and could not be drawn back. He had to wait until the man of God restored it (1 Kgs 13:4-6). And there is another short drama at the Jordan building site. An ax head that fell into the water cannot be recovered, but since it is borrowed there is a need to retrieve it. When the prophet makes it rise, the man stretches out his hand and recovers it (2 Kgs 6:5-7). This is one of those cases where, for the present writer at least, it is difficult to be clear about what relationship, if any, exists between the texts.

Both accounts go on to describe longer dramas involving food and the word of God. The man of God, disobedient to God's word concerning food and then killed by a lion, is noticed by the people going into the town (1 Kgs 13:11-34, esp. vv. 23-26). And in a much more public setting—that of the Aramean wars—the officer who had been cynical about the prophetic provision of food is killed by the people coming out of the town (2 Kgs 6:24–7:20, esp. 7:16-20). The primary focus in both texts is not on the food but on the need to rely on the word of God.

But the schism story has other episodes, including turning armies around and sending them home. A man of God persuades a vast Judean army, intent on invading the northern kingdom, to go home (1 Kgs 12:21-24). And when the northern kingdom is threatened by various Aramean forces these forces are sent back, first by Elisha (2 Kgs 6:23) and later, in a different manner, by YHWH (2 Kgs 7:6-7).

At this point the Elijah-Elisha account of the Aramean wars (2 Kings 6–8) involves a synthesizing of various texts. The feeding and turning back of the initial Aramean force, for instance, seems to involve a blending of 1 Kings 12 (turning back an army, 12:21-24) and 1 Kings 13 (bringing someone aside for food, 13:14-19).

The subsequent story about Jeroboam's son—first his sickness and then the foretelling of his death (1 Kgs 14:1-20)—is reflected in the later story referring to the Shunammitess's son (2 Kgs 8:1-6) and in Elisha's foretelling of the death of Ben-haded (2 Kgs 8:7-13).

The contribution of this five-chapter schism-centered text (1 Kgs 12:1–16:28) is not to be overrated; as implied earlier (pp. 37–38) it provides just one component to the account of the Aramean wars (2 Kings 6–8). The Elijah-Elisha narrative has filtered the schism-centered text and has used it, particularly its prophetic emphasis, to shape a new text, an account that comprises other components and which follows the requirements of its own narrative cohesion, including, for instance, continuity with earlier Aramean wars (in 1 Kings 20).

MURDEROUS FALL AND IDOLATRY: ISRAEL'S FALL (2 KINGS 14–17) AND JEHU'S DESTRUCTION OF ISRAEL'S HOUSE (2 KINGS 9–10)

The final major section of the Primary History consists of the account of the fall of the two kingdoms of the north and south (2 Kings 14–25), and it is this climactic account which underlies the longest sequence in the Elijah-Elisha narrative—the final five chapters (2 Kings 9–13), a sequence that is dramatic and essentially unbroken. As already indicated, these five final chapters are held together by Elisha's initial action of designating Jehu and by all the consequences, north and south, which flow from Jehu's deathly purging of his kingdom.

First, the north (2 Kings 14–17, and 2 Kings 9–10). The Primary History's four-chapter account of the events leading to the fall of Israel is quite complex (2 Kings 14–17). In particular there are summaries, partly formulaic, of at least ten reigns, some of them Judean (14:1–17:4). But amid the complexity of the reigns in Israel there is a pattern which is disturbingly steady: assassination of the king (15:10, 14, 25, 30). Then comes King Hoshea, the murderer of King Pekah (15:30), and it seems for a while that he will survive. But his double-dealing leads to overthrow, imprisonment, and massive deportment, thus ending the northern kingdom of Israel (17:1-6).

The final chapter concerning Israel's fall (2 Kgs 17:7-41) gives the underlying reason for the disaster, namely idolatry, including worship of Baal (17:7-12, 14-18), and it indicates that Israel had been warned through the prophets (17:13).

This complex account of Israel's end (chs. 14–17) is reflected in the story of Jehu (2 Kings 9–10). While the Jehu narrative is quite distinctive and contains its own specific sources, it also distills some of the key elements of the longer text, particularly the murdering of Israel's royal line, the underlying problem of Baal-related idolatry, and the role of the prophets.

The amount of attention given to the prophets varies greatly from one text to another. In the basic account of Israel's fall (2 Kings 14–17) the reference to the prophets, while significant, is small and is set near the end (17:13). But in the Elijah-Elisha narrative, with its general emphasis on prophecy, the role of the prophets is highlighted and set at the beginning: it is the prophets who inaugurate Jehu's murderous overthrow of the royal house (9:1-10).

The Jehu drama acts as an interpreter: it crystallizes the nature of a whole succession of northern reigns. The prolonged deviance of the north, particularly as concerns worship, becomes vivid in Jezebel and her Baalites. And the apparently endemic northern violence becomes graphic in Jehu's purges. Within the Primary History as a whole, Jehu's purging of the Temple is an intimation that the kingdom of the north is coming to an end.

Next, the south.

Defeating Death and Reforming the Temple: Hezekiah/Josiah (2 Kings 18–25) and Joash/Elisha (2 Kings 11–13)

Precisely when the Primary History first focuses exclusively on the south (in its concluding chapters, 2 King 18–25), the Elijah-Elisha narrative makes a comparable move: for the first time it switches attention essentially to the south (in its concluding chapters, 2 Kings 11–13). Thus the final emphasis, both in the Primary History and in its interpretive synthesis, is on Judah.

The change brings relief. Despite much that is negative, including murderous Manasseh (ch. 21), the eight-chapter account of the final kings of Judea (2 Kings 18–25) is dominated by two figures who are immensely positive: Hezekiah, who survived both Sennacherib's army and deathly illness (2 Kings 18–20), and Josiah, the young king who, faced with the discovery of the Law in the temple, inaugurated a bold reform (2 Kings 22–23).

The end of the Elijah-Elisha narrative (2 Kings 11–13) is likewise dominated by two immensely positive figures: the young reforming Joash, and Elisha, whose illness and death turn into a source of life. As the apparently dying Hezekiah turned away death, so, even more wondrously, did Elisha.

There is, of course, a shadow side. Manasseh's crimes included making his own son pass through fire (1 Kgs 21:6) and committing many murders (1 Kgs 21:16: shedding so much innocent blood as to fill the whole of Jerusalem). And this is reflected in the Elijah-Elisha narrative: the Jerusalem episode begins with murder, with Athaliah's killing of Judah's royal stock (11:1). But, taken as a whole, the conclusions of the two narratives are positive.

Some of the main connections between the texts—the end of the Primary History and the end of the Elisha story—are as follows:

The framework text, the text which provides a foundation for much of the Elisha-related account (at least for 2 Kings 11–12), consists largely of Josiah's reform (2 Kgs 22:1–23:30), an account from near the *end* of the underlying block (2 Kings 18–25; generally the foundation text has been taken from near the beginning).

There is a major difference between the two reforms. Josiah's reform is sparked by the discovery of a book; Joash's springs from the revealing of the person himself. Like the book, he himself had in effect been hidden in the Temple; his emergence, like that of the book, sparked a renewal centered on covenant and Temple (2 Kings 23; 2 Kgs 11:17-18; 12:1-21). Unlike Josiah, however, who spent much energy on removing the rival cult centers which distracted from the Temple, Joash concentrates on improving the running of the Temple itself.

Given the larger relationship between the Primary History and the Elijah-Elisha narrative, the account of Joash's reform (2 Kgs 11:17-18; 12:1-21) constitutes an interpretation of the reform of Josiah. This interpretation, while making no reference to a book (the book of the Law), highlights more clearly three basic factors: the human person (Joash, cared for from babyhood), the Temple (also cared for), and the covenant. The emphasis on a covenant is set at the beginning, in the covenant involving YHWH, king, and people (1 Kgs 11:17); it reappears again at the very end, recalling Abraham, Isaac, and Jacob (2 Kgs 13:23).

Incidentally, there is no explicit reference in 2 Kings 11–13 to the covenant of Moses. However, covenant references in 2 Kings 11–13 extend from Abraham to the king, and perhaps this broad emphasis on covenant as such implicitly includes Moses.

The Hezekiah text (chs. 18–20) is first very public, dealing with Sennacherib's military might (chs. 18–19), and then relatively private, dealing with illness and virtual death (ch. 20). In using all this

Hezekiah material to help describe the death of Elisha (13:14-21) the Elisha narrative gives priority to Hezekiah's encounter with death (ch. 20), but it also distills the military section (chs. 18–19), thus injecting a military dimension—weapons—into the scene of Elisha's death.

At one level the illnesses of Hezekiah and Elisha require no special explanation. One recovers and the other dies. But there is more. Hezekiah not only recovers, there is a sign or miracle: the day's sun-shadow turns backward (20:8-11). And Elisha not only dies, his bones give life to a person who is being carried to burial (13:21). Thus both texts suggest that death is being turned back in a way that breaks normal patterns of expectation. There is a successful challenging of the implacable march toward sunset and burial.

The implication of turning back the sunset is obscure. But then, in turning back the march toward burial, obscurity fades. Here, in the death of Elisha, an idea which has hovered intermittently and enigmatically over the Primary History finally becomes graphically clear: there is recovery from death, in fact a form of rising from the dead.

In using the last chapter of the Primary History—the death-filled Babylonian invasion (25:1-26) and the hopeful sketch of the semi-restored king (25:27-30)—the Elisha account, at this point at least, distilled the invasion text to an absolute minimum. The only echo of invasion is in the reference to Moabite raiders (13:20).

But the suggestion of hope, the Primary History's final word (2 Kgs 25:27-30), provides the inspiration for a final word which is yet more positive. While the Primary History at this point bases its hope on the goodness of the Babylonian king (literally, the king "spoke good things [*tōbôt*] to him," 25:28), the Elijah-Elisha narrative portrays the re-emergence of the grace and compassion of God, a compassion which builds not on changing whim but on the ancient covenant with Abraham, Isaac, and Jacob (13:23). It is a compassion which, at the end of the Elijah-Elisha narrative, leads to the restoration of Israel's cities, implicitly to a form of restoration of Israel itself (13:25). The city may have fallen but at another level Israel's cities will be restored.

Here too, in expressing final hope, the Elijah-Elisha narrative brings clarity to the enigmatic Primary History. While the recovery of Jerusalem's former king to a certain dignity may seem ambiguous (2 Kgs 25:27-30), there is no ambiguity about the recovery that follows the death of Elisha (2 Kgs 13:22-25): on the basis of an age-old covenant there is a threefold victory and a restoration of Israel's cities.

CONCLUSION

The analysis given here is quite incomplete. Just as this chapter develops what was done in the chapter which preceded, so, ideally, this chapter itself should now be developed at much greater length. For the moment that is not possible.

Yet what has been done here is significant. Like a trench across a great archaeological site, this brief analysis provides a strong indication of the larger reality. In particular it confirms the interim conclusion from the preceding chapter. On the one hand, the Elijah-Elisha narrative has major persistent similarities with the larger history (Genesis-Kings). On the other hand, the differences between the texts, huge though they are, follow certain consistent patterns. In particular, the larger history's emphasis on kings and armies has given way to the primacy of prophecy.

The implication is clear. The logic which for long has concluded that part of the Elijah-Elisha narrative reflects Moses now indicates that that narrative reflects the whole Primary History.

DEFINING THE RELATIONSHIP

It is not clear how to describe what the Elijah-Elisha narrative does to the larger history, what category or term to use. Is it, for instance, some form of rewriting? A prophetic re-envisioning?

The useful term "interpretive interlude" may be borrowed from Alan Culpepper, his way of describing the sequence of the blind man and the good shepherd (John 9:1–10:21).[4] A somewhat similar concept, "hermeneutic center," occurs in Robert Polzin: he sug-

---

[4] Alan Culpepper, *Anatomy of the Fourth Gospel* (Philadelphia: Fortress Press, 1983) 93.

gests that "2 Samuel 12 is the hermeneutic center of the entire royal history, as 1 Samuel 1–7 was its interpretive introduction."[5]

After further investigation it has seemed best to use the term "interpretive synthesis," at least as a working hypothesis. This maintains the ideas of interpretation (Culpepper) or hermeneutics (Polzin), but it also reflects something proper to the Elijah-Elisha narrative—the systematic way it distills and mirrors the larger history.

The idea of a literary mirror is not new. As indicated by François Bovon[6] this idea corresponds to the process known as *mise en abyme*—a literary convention in which part of a text "functions as [a] mirror or microcosm of the [larger] text."[7] The basic idea of a *mise en abyme* is illustrated in art by Jan van Eyck's *The Arnolfini Wedding:* the painting includes a dark convex mirror which reflects the larger scene, but from another perspective.[8]

In this context, the word *abyme* (a variant spelling of *abîme*) derives not from any profound idea of an "abyss" but from technical usage in heraldry. When, within the complex designs on a heraldic shield, there is one figure which is central but somehow apart, not touching the others, it is said to be *en abyme.*[9]

Aspects of such relationships—apart yet central—occur even within Genesis. The story of Judah and Tamar (Genesis 38) stands

[5] Robert Polzin, *David and the Deuteronomist: A Literary Study of the Deuteronomic History,* Part 3 (Bloomington and Indianapolis: Indiana University, 1993) 120.

[6] François Bovon, conversation with author, Cambridge, Mass., Feb. 18, 1997.

[7] Lucien Dällenbach, *Mirrors and After: Five Essays on Literary Theory and Criticism* (New York: City University of New York, 1986) 9; see Lucien Dällenbach, *Le récit spéculaire. Contribution a l'étude de la mise en abyme* (Paris: Seuil, 1977).

[8] Dällenbach, *Mirrors and After,* 8.

[9] Dällenbach, *Le récit spéculaire,* 17. The phrase *mise en abyme* also expresses the phenomenon of images that progress downward indefinitely, as, for instance, with facing mirrors, or, more properly, when a picture of the artist at work contains a smaller picture of the artist at work, and so on (Diana Culbertson, conversation with author, Jacob's Field, Cleveland, Ohio, May 22, 1997).

apart from the Joseph story at one level, yet at another it is central: it distills into one vivid episode the whole complex drama of the deviation and conversion of Judah (Gen 37:26-27; 43:3-10; 44:18-34; cf. 49:8-12).

The relationship between the large text and the smaller interpretive text is not fixed; "the degree of analogy . . . can give rise to various forms of reduplication."[10]

The form of reduplication which occurs in the Elijah-Elisha narrative is simultaneously faithful and innovative. The essence of the entire Genesis-Kings history is mirrored dutifully and in the same order, but the long accounts of the Primary History are reshaped, filtered as it were through the lens of prophets and prophecy. A prophetic element had already been present in Genesis-Kings, at least implicitly. But in the Elijah-Elisha narrative it comes clearly to the fore. The events recounted in the Primary History were first set in motion by God's creative word. At the end, in the interpretive mirror of the Elijah-Elisha narrative, the presence of that word becomes more tangible. History, even at its worst, somehow expresses or reflects God's word.

[10] Dällenbach, *Mirrors and After,* 10.

CHAPTER 4

THE CENTRAL ROLE OF
THE ELIJAH-ELISHA NARRATIVE:
A REINTERPRETATION OF
THE LEADING SCRIPTURES

In the history of interpretation few works have been as bold as the Elijah-Elisha narrative. It has taken the leading Scriptures—the unforgettable foundational saga that runs across century after century, from creation to the fall of Jerusalem—and, while staying within that saga, has brought it to a new level, shifting the emphasis from wars to words, from law to prophecy, from the external to the internal. Not that the creation-Jerusalem saga is all external, or the Elijah-Elisha narrative all internal. Far from it. But the change in emphasis is considerable. The glory of old, of patriarchs and lawmakers, of conquerors and kings, has been replaced by a glory which, while vivid and powerful, sometimes even harsh, is focused with fresh clarity on the central elusive reality of God's word and on the implications of that word for humanity.

From this interpretation the following features stand out: a shift in genre, a clarifying of content, an interpretive synthesizing, and, yet, a role that remains within the larger text (within the Primary History).

GENRE: A SHIFT FROM HISTORY
TOWARD BIOGRAPHY

As the terminology suggests, the Primary History, despite its immense complexity, belongs primarily to the genre of history. But, beginning with Jacob (Gen 25:19–50:26), there are times when this history becomes biography, at least to some degree. One of the basic features of the Elijah-Elisha narrative is that even though it is reflecting the history as a whole, it shifts the overall emphasis somewhat from history toward biography. The long flow of centuries and great leaders, especially kings, gives way in Elijah and Elisha to a greater emphasis on two people, who, despite their prophetic gifts, seem closer than kings to ordinary human life. The Elijah-Elisha narrative is not biographic in the full sense—it is still largely governed both by the preceding history and by the overarching emphasis on the word—but the shift toward biography is significant.

A CLARIFYING OF CONTENT

In contrast to the sometimes overwhelming complexity and richness of the Primary History, the Elijah-Elisha narrative highlights certain key features, features which flow into one another and thus into a fresh unity. Some of the main features are as follows:

THE WORD

"Words are dynamite," a courageous Northern Ireland politician once said about the need to be careful in speech. This saying is even more true in dealing with the word of God: from the beginning of creation the divine word makes and breaks. It is essentially positive—both God's word and genuine attentiveness to God uplift people—but, for someone set on evil, God's word can also be a radical challenge. The multi-faceted richness of God's word is perhaps the single most important idea in the Elijah-Elisha narrative. From the God-given pattern of command-and-compliance at the beginning, during the drought (1 Kgs 17:1-16), to the analogous Elisha-given pattern at the end (about taking the weapons,

2 Kgs 13:14-19; cf. 11:4-11), the role of the word is central to the entire narrative.

The Prophet

Second only to the word is the one who often bears the word, namely the prophet. Generally this is Elijah or Elisha. But they have no monopoly; the narrative is more interested in the message, the divine word, than in specific human messengers. Yet these two do have a central role. Amid the turbulence of history and the multiplicity of prophets, even authentic prophets—for many are false—they stand out and give a certain stability and tone to the narrative.

Elijah and Elisha together form a kind of prophetic synthesis; "they provided the fullest account available of the lives of Yahwistic prophets."[1]

The Primary Effect of the Word:
Life, Including Healing

The primary goal of the word is not to dazzle or destroy, it is to give life and, when life is endangered, to heal and nourish. In the drought, God's word nourishes Elijah; Elijah's word in turn nourishes and enlivens the widow and her son (1 Kings 17). More than any other extended Hebrew narrative, the account of Elijah and Elisha emphasizes healing.

Life, Including Life beyond Death

What emerges from reflective study is that Elijah and Elisha are neither collection points for sundry legends nor marginal eccentrics. Rather they are the divinely-mandated agents who engage the substantive questions of life and death. The primary issue at the beginning of the Elijah story (1 Kings 17–19) is the struggle against death.[2] The primary issue in much of the Elisha

---

[1] Robert Carroll, "The Elijah-Elisha Sagas: Some Remarks on Prophetic Succession in Ancient Israel," *VT* 19 (1969) 413.

[2] Alan Hauser and Russel Gregory, *From Carmel to Horeb: Elijah in Crisis,* Bible and Literature 19 (Sheffield: Almond, 1990) 80–2.

text, particularly in Elisha's encounters with Aramean soldiers and armies (2 Kings 6–8), is some form of salvation.[3] This is no petty literature.

The Elijah-Elisha narrative, while accepting the stark reality of death and burial (at the end Elisha is buried), nonetheless wrestles at various points not only with death but with the question of life beyond death. As the narrative progresses, the extent of the miracles intensifies: raising the widow's son, dead or near-dead (1 Kgs 17:17-24); raising the Shunammitess's son, fully dead (2 Kgs 4:18-20); the rising of a dead man who is virtually buried (2 Kgs 13:21).

The engagement with death is seen most splendidly in the centerpiece, at the end of the first drama: God takes Elijah up to heaven (2 Kgs 2:1, 11). This event is not completely without precedent. The Primary History, at its beginning, alluded cryptically to such an event when Enoch was taken by God (Gen 5:24). But the Elijah-Elisha narrative spells it out in vivid detail. The implication is of someone passing through death.

To some degree the emphasis on overcoming death seems to set the Elijah-Elisha narrative at odds with the rest of the Primary History. The episode of raising the widow's son, for instance, when Elijah prays that the *nephesh* return to the boy's body (1 Kgs 17:21-22), uses *nephesh* ("soul/breath") as apparently indicating a soul that is separable (1 Kgs 17:22), a sense different from the generally accepted meaning of *nephesh*.[4]

However, this sense of *nephesh*—as in some way separable— is not completely new. A study of several diverse texts, including Genesis and the raising of the widow's son (1 Kings 17), led James Barr to a similar view:

> I submit . . . that it seems probable that in certain contexts the *nephesh* is *not,* as much present opinion favours, a unity of body and soul, a totality of personality comprising all these elements; it

[3] Rick Dale Moore, *God Saves: Lessons from the Elisha Stories,* JSOTSS 95 (Sheffield: Sheffield Academic, 1990) 128–33.

[4] Thomas Overholt, *Cultural Anthropology and the Old Testament,* Guides to Biblical Scholarship (Minneapolis: Fortress Press, 1996) 29–38, esp. 32–3.

is rather, in these contexts, a superior controlling center which accompanies, expresses and directs the existence of that totality, and one which, especially, provides the life to the whole. Because it is the life-giving element, it is difficult to conceive that it itself will die. It may simply return to God, life to the source of life. Otherwise it may still exist, and the thought of its being brought down to Sheol, or being killed, is intolerable. It is *particularly* the thought of the envelopment of the *nephesh,* in the sense of "soul," in Sheol that is hateful. With the recognition of this fact the gate to immortality lies open. I do not say that the Hebrews, in early times, "believed in the immortality of the soul." But they did have terms, distinctions and beliefs upon which such a position could be built and was in fact eventually built.[5]

To some degree, then, it is arguable that the Elijah-Elisha narrative, rather than opposing the Primary History's sense of death, is simply bringing out clearly what the history had implied. As the meaning of Enoch's disappearance becomes clearer through Elijah's ascent, so other puzzling episodes involving death take on a new meaning.

Kings, Armies, and Chariots

The immediate context for the Elijah-Elisha narrative is one of kings. The very books are generally called 1 and 2 Kings. But in this narrative the role of kings and armies is demystified. They sometimes boast easily (1 Kgs 22:3-4, 10; 2 Kgs 3:7-8), but having boasted they accomplish almost nothing, at least nothing positive. The figure of Jehu, warrior supreme, gives armies an even worse name (2 Kings 9–10).

The Elijah-Elisha narrative, however, not only deflates kings and armies, it also steals their thunder. It takes chariots and horses, one of the greatest symbols of political and military power, and places them within the service of God. The real chariot of Israel is not that on the field of battle, not the bloodied chariot of Ahab (1 Kings 22), but the fiery chariot that carries away Elijah

---

[5] James Barr, *The Garden of Eden and the Hope of Immortality* (Minneapolis: Fortress Press, 1992) 37–43, esp. 42–3.

(2 Kings 2; cf. 6:15-17). It is Elijah, rather than any king, who encapsulates Israel's true power. Elisha too, even in his illness, in some sense does likewise (2 Kgs 13:14). And it is the dying Elisha who gives power to the weapons of king Joash (2 Kgs 13:15-19). The implication: true kingly power resides not with kings but with the word of God.

WOMEN

In addition to being critical of men at their most powerful and boastful—as kings and warriors—the Elijah-Elisha narrative also seems critical of women, or at least of women who are as power-hungry as ranking men. In the whole Elijah-Elisha narrative the only women in positions of obvious power are Jezebel and Athaliah, both killers (1 Kgs 18:4; 2 Kgs 11:1). This seems to be an extremely harsh portrayal, but it is primarily part of the larger criticism of people in political power, rather than a criticism of women as such. In the most dramatic showdown between people in power, the confrontation between Jezebel and Jehu (2 Kgs 9:30-37), there is a sense in which they are well met—she adorned, he armed, both killers. But, despite being dishonored, she loses with class, whereas he, the victor, seems utterly brutish (except perhaps within a dehumanized warrior ethos).

Apart from this suspicion of militarized political power—male or female—there are two key facets to the Elijah-Elisha narratives' presentation of women. On the one hand, no woman is mentioned among the prophets. There is no Deborah (Judges 4) or Huldah (2 Kgs 22:11-22). The groups of prophets consist largely of brotherhoods, apparently all men (for example, 2 Kgs 2:3-7, 15-18).

On the other hand, the women who do appear—representatives apparently of the vast majority of women, whether poor or rich—are sensitive, dignified, and strong. This is true not only of the woman to whom Elijah travels (1 Kings 17), but especially of the two women met by Elisha (2 Kings 4). The latter case is particularly significant because there appears to be a deliberate contrast between the men and women respectively in the two panels of the diptych (2 Kings 3 and 4), and, as already noted, there is also a contrast between the Shunammitess and her husband (2 Kgs

4:18-24). By and large the women do well in the comparison. The woman of Shunem exercises a double leadership—through her force of character and through her role as benefactor.

THE TEMPLE AND PRIESTS

In the nature of the narrative—set in northern Israel, there is little mention of the Temple and priests. Yet, in the opening diptych, and from the very beginning, authentic worship is an issue. The Elijah story is introduced with a picture of the deviant worship of Baal and the murderous sacrificing of sons (1 Kgs 16:32-34), and the issue on Mount Carmel is the authenticity of worship (1 Kgs 18:16-40).

In the final diptych the action is guided significantly by a priest, Jehoida, and the concern is not so much with the condemnation of false worship as with the promotion of worship that is true—in the Temple (2 Kings 11–12).

Hence, despite the relatively small amount of space given to the Temple—especially in contrast to Chronicles—there is an implication, first and last, that the role of (Temple) worship is important.

POOR AND RICH

The first person whom Elijah encounters is a woman gathering sticks (1 Kgs 17:10). It is she, rather than anyone of wealth or prestige, who seems most attentive to the word and who first draws life from it. At other moments too it is those who are relatively poor or powerless who seem most sensitive to the word, for instance, the indebted widow (2 Kgs 4:1-4), the slave girl (2 Kgs 5:2-3), and the servants (2 Kgs 5:13). Yet Elijah and Elisha have no antipathy to the rich as such. Elijah is patient with Obadiah, the master of Ahab's palace (1 Kgs 18:1-15). Apparently Elisha himself had been quite wealthy—plowing with twelve yoke of oxen (1 Kgs 19:19). The Shunammitess, with her spare wealth, was hesitant yet ultimately attentive (2 Kgs 4:8-37). Likewise wealthy Naaman; despite initial superficiality and pride, he learned to listen (2 Kgs 5:1-14).

The attentiveness of the Elijah-Elisha narrative to the marginalized is seen most clearly in its attitude to lepers. In every case—Naaman, Gehazi, and the four outside Samaria (2 Kgs 5:1-27; 7:3-11; 8:4-6)—their role as afflicted is not allowed to overshadow their more basic status as human beings. In fact, the lepers, instead of being marginalized from the truth of God's word, appear in the end to be particularly close to it, and in varying ways they bring that good word to others, even into the presence of kings (2 Kgs 5:15-19; 7:9-11; 8:4-6). The Elijah-Elisha treatment of the lepers indicates an attitude that is radically inclusive.

AN INTERPRETIVE SYNTHESIS

The purpose of this study is not to travel a long journey but, along with researchers such as Patricia Dutcher-Wells, Rick Dale Moore, Alan Hauser, Russel Gregory, and Marsha White, to indicate a sense of direction. The Elijah-Elisha narrative is not just a collection of legends. It is a sophisticated literary unity, combining both coherent internal relationships and a massive external relationship to the rest of Genesis-Kings. And, more important than its literary features—but built on them—it is a major theological text. Omitting shoals of details, it not only synthesizes the Primary History but does so in a way which rethinks the great issues of life and death, of word and war, of politics and prophets, and it brings these issues to a new level of depth and clarity. The centerpiece picture of Elijah's ascent is not a legendary curio. It is a climactic evocation of the destiny of humankind.

A NARRATIVE APART, YET WITHIN

The Elijah-Elisha narrative is not a distinct book. It is an integral part of the Primary History itself. Like many a church tower, it must have been virtually the last part of the Primary History to have been built,[6] but it is so integrated that, like most towers, it

---

[6] On the possibly later composition of Mosaic law, see Calum M. Carmichael, "'An Eye for an Eye, and a Tooth for a Tooth': The History of Formula," *Law, Morality, and Religion: Global Perspectives,* ed. Alan Watson (Berkeley: University of California Press, 1996) 1–29. Calum M. Carmichael, *Law and Narrative in the Bible. The Evidence of the Deuteronomic Laws and the Decalogue* (Ithaca, N.Y./London: Cornell University Press, 1985) esp. 17.

must have been planned from the beginning. The introduction to the reign of Ahab (16:29-34), for instance, is both the inextricable background for the Elijah-Elisha narrative and also a close-knit part of the larger chain of kings and their reigns. Likewise Jehu (2 Kings 9–10): he is interwoven with both the Elisha episodes and the larger framework of kings.

Yet, again like the church tower, the Elijah-Elisha narrative stands apart. In fact, this perception of being somehow apart or late is one of the most widespread scholarly opinions concerning the nature and origin of the Elijah-Elisha material.[7]

Given this separateness, it is tempting to set the Elijah-Elisha narrative in opposition, even strong opposition, to the rest of Genesis-Kings. And it would be easy then to imagine a background of two opposing social groups.

Tensions in society are not to be excluded, but reconstructing them on the basis of tensions in the text is hazardous. This is particularly so since the two parts of the text—the general history and its interpretive mirror—are so inextricably interwoven. Hence, rather than speak of opposition, still less of two opposing social groups—opposition often entails deliberate deafness—it seems better to speak of dialectic and dialogue. In contrast to much modern thought with its implicit idea of truth as monological or simple ("Just get the facts"), some great literature, including an extensive amount of biblical literature, has apparently been constructed with a different model of truth—truth as dialogical.[8] The Elijah-Elisha narrative is in strong dialogue with the rest of the Primary History. It does not deny its existence, its battles and its beauty, but it provides an alternative view, one which gives a clearer sense of the reality of God's word.

---

[7] Thomas Römer and Albert de Pury, "L'historiographie deutéronomiste (HD). Histoire de la recherche et enjeu du debat," *Israël construit son histoire. L'historiographie deutéronomiste à la lumière des recherches récentes,* ed. Albert de Pury et al. (Geneva: Labor et Fides, 1996) 113.

[8] On the concept of truth as dialogical, rather than monological, and on the presence of that concept in biblical narrative, see Carol Newsom, "Bakhtin, the Bible, and Dialogic Truth," *JR* 76 (1996).

NOTE: A FURTHER REINTERPRETATION:
THE CHRONICLER

The boldness of the Elijah-Elisha narrative is partly repeated in the work of the Chronicler. Here too the Primary History is largely rewritten within a relatively short work, within the sixty-five chapters of 1 and 2 Chronicles. Like the author of the Elijah-Elisha narrative, the Chronicler combined diverse modes of adaptation into a coherent authorial process.[9] The detail of their two respective works—the fabric and theme of their narratives—is vastly different, but, in the boldness of the basic project, there is significant continuity. The shape of history, no matter how sacred, could be redrawn.

---

[9] John Kleinig, "Recent Research in Chronicles," *Currents in Research* 2 (1994) esp. 47–9.

CHAPTER 5

A LITERARY MODEL FOR THE GOSPELS

The literary background of the Gospels has always been a puzzle. From the time writing was invented, ancient literary works almost invariably used precedents—they imitated or adapted various aspects of earlier works[1]—but it is not clear what literary precedents or models the evangelists used.

Part of the answer lies in the Greco-Roman world. To some degree, the evangelists incorporated features of the known world's mainstream narratives, particularly some features of history and biography.[2] But despite showing many affinities, some quite

---

[1] W. G. Lambert, *Babylonian Wisdom Literature* (Oxford: Clarendon Press, 1960) 2, 6; Thomas Brodie, "Greco-Roman Imitation of Texts as a Partial Guide to Luke's Use of Sources," *Luke-Acts: New Perspectives from the Society of Biblical Literature Seminar,* ed. C. H. Talbert, 17–46 (New York: Crossroad, 1984).

[2] Charles Talbert, *What Is a Gospel? The Genre of the Canonical Gospels* (Philadelphia: Fortress Press, 1977); Philip Shuler, *A Genre for the Gospels: The Biographical Character of Matthew* (Philadelphia: Fortress Press, 1982); Richard Burridge, *What Are the Gospels? A Comparison with Greco-Roman Biography,* SNTSMS 70 (Cambridge: Cambridge University Press, 1992); Gregory Sterling, *Historiography and Self-Definition: Josephos, Luke-Acts and Apologetic Historiography,* NTS 44 (London/New York/Köln: Brill, 1992); Adela Yarbro Collins,

significant, the Greco-Roman world does not have one particular account which by itself provides a credible model for the composition of the Gospels.

In the Hebrew Scriptures, however, particularly as translated into Greek (the Septuagint), there are narratives which go far in providing a model. Raymond Brown[3] has indicated that the Gospels were partly modeled on the prophetic biographies, particularly the account of Elisha and his miracles. In varying degrees, others have agreed with the essence of this idea.[4]

The purpose here is to corroborate Brown's proposal, in particular to make it more precise: the foundational model for the development of the Gospels was not just the account of Elisha's miracles, it was the entire Elijah-Elisha narrative.

EXPLICIT REFERENCES

While Elisha's name occurs only once in the New Testament (in the Nazareth speech, Luke 4:27), Elijah's name occurs twenty-nine times, all but two in the Gospels. Even at a superficial level, therefore, Elijah is an obvious part of the Gospels' fabric.

Within this obvious usage the pattern is not clear. On some occasions Elijah is associated with John the Baptist—suggesting that John is the returned Elijah (cf. Luke 1:17; Mark 9:10-12; Matt 17:10-12; 11:14), yet in John's Gospel the Baptist denies that he is Elijah (John 1:21-25).

The Beginning of the Gospel: Probings of Mark in Context (Minneapolis: Fortress Press, 1992); Christopher Bryan, *A Preface to Mark: Notes on the Gospel in Its Literary and Cultural Settings* (New York/Oxford: Oxford University Press, 1993).

[3] Raymond Brown, "Jesus and Elisha," *Perspective* 12 (1971) 98–9.

[4] Talbert, *What Is a Gospel?;* Martin Hengel, *Acts and the History of Earliest Christianity* (Philadelphia: Fortress Press, 1980) 30–2; David Barr and Judith Wentling, "The Conventions of Classical Biography and the Genre of Luke-Acts: A Preliminary Study," paper presented at the SBL/CBA regional meeting, Duquesne University, Pittsburgh, Pa., April 1980; see Yarbro Collins, *The Beginning of the Gospel,* 27–36.

On other occasions Elijah is associated not with John the Baptist but with Jesus. Elijah is a model, along with Elisha, for Jesus' ministry (Luke 4:25-26), and he is a companion, along with Moses, of Jesus' Transfiguration (Mark 9:3, 4; Matt 17:3, 4; Luke 9:30, 33). But again there is an opposite tendency: despite the crowds' opinions, Jesus is not Elijah (Mark 6:15; 8:28; Matt 16:14; Luke 9:8, 19). When these references are taken on their own and used as a direct basis for history they tend inevitably to generate confusion.

OTHER KINDS OF REFERENCES

The dependence Brown referred to was not just to isolated references; it was to the whole genre of the Elisha account. Other researchers too have moved beyond explicit references; they have realized with varying degrees of clarity that the explicit references, apart from possibly having a historical dimension, are also just a small part of a deep engagement with the Scriptures. This larger involvement appears in several studies on the roles of Elijah and Elisha in the New Testament.[5]

---

[5] These studies include, in chronological order: Gerhard Hartmann, *Der aufbau des Markusevangeliums,* NTAbh 17, nos. 2–3 (Münster: Aschendorff, 1936); P. Dabeck, "Siehe, es erschienen Moses und Elias," *Bib* 23 (1942) 175–89; Marie-Emile Boismard, "Elie dans le Nouveau Testament," *Elie le prophète, I: Selon les Ecritures et les traditions chrétiennes,* Etudes Carmélitanes (Bruges: Desclée de Brouwer, 1956) 116–28; Barnabas Lindars, "Elijah, Elisha and the Gospel Miracles," *Miracles,* ed. C.F.D. Moule, 63–79 (London: Bowbray; New York: Morehouse-Barlow, 1965); Walter Wink, *John the Baptist in the Gospel Tradition,* SNTSMS 7 (Cambridge: Cambridge University Press, 1968); J. D. Dubois, "La Figure d'Elie dans la Perspective Lucanienne," *RHPR* 53 (1973) 155–76; Paul Hinnebusch, *Jesus, the New Elijah* (Ann Arbor, Mich.: Servant Books, 1978); D. Gerald Bostock, "Jesus as the New Elisha," *ExpTim* 91 (1980) 39–41; Wolfgang Roth, *Hebrew Gospel: Cracking the Code of Mark* (Yorktown Heights, N.Y.: Meyer Stone Books, 1988); Gerhard Dautzenberg, "Elija im Markusevangelium," *The Four Gospels, 1992: Festschrift Frans Neirynck,* BETL 100, ed. F. Van Segbroeck et al., 1077–94 (Leuven: Leuven University/Peeters, 1992).

The debate at times becomes obscure and unconvincing, but overall it is significant. It indicates that if one takes time to work closely with the texts, rather than worry prematurely about historical conclusions, patterns of deliberate literary affinity do begin to emerge.

However, rather than speak in generalities, it is better to look at two specific cases: Luke-Acts and Mark.

ELIJAH-ELISHA AND LUKE-ACTS

At first sight Luke-Acts may appear very different from the Elijah-Elisha narrative. Luke's prologue (1:1-4), for instance, has a Hellenistic tone which is far removed from the Elijah scene, and something similar is true of aspects of Luke-Acts as a whole. For example, Luke-Acts has a special affinity with Hellenistic history,[6] and this affinity seems to set it in a different category from the prophecy-oriented account of Elijah and Elisha.

But just as Christianity was open, in principle, both to Jew and Greek, so Christian literature could combine what was Hellenistic with what was Jewish. It is generally agreed, first of all, that Luke imitated the Greek Old Testament, adapting various aspects of its vocabulary, style, genre, and content.[7] Nor is Luke's method haphazard; rather, "the author tends towards a treatment of the Scriptures which we would nowadays call systematic."[8] In Sterling's summary:

> The LXX was of central importance for Luke-Acts. It provided the language for sections of the work, the concept of history which pervades it, and may have supplied some of the forms themselves. More important than this is the realization that our author conceived of his work as the *continuation* of the LXX. His deliberate

[6] See esp. Sterling, *Historiography and Self-Definition,* 369–89.

[7] For detailed references, see Thomas Brodie, "Towards Unravelling Luke's Use of the Old Testament: Luke 7:11-17 as an *Imitatio* of 1 Kings 17:17-24," *New Testament Studies* 32 (1986) 249.

[8] Bart Koet, *Five Studies on Interpretation of Scripture in Luke-Acts,* SNTA 14 (Leuven: Leuven University/Peeters, 1989) 141.

composition in Septuagintal Greek and the conviction that his story was the fulfilment of the promises of the OT imply that as a continuation, Luke-Acts represents *sacred narrative.*[9]

Luke therefore used the Septuagint as a whole.

It is possible, however, to be more precise: Luke made particular use of the Elijah-Elisha narrative. The similarities here are not just around vocabulary, style, and genre. They involve features that are quite specific. These features revolve around three basic concerns: central themes, basic structures, and specific episodes.

CENTRAL THEMES

The thematic link is not something minor. Luke-Acts has a special emphasis on themes that are foundational to the Elijah-Elisha narrative: the role of prophecy and the word. More than in other Gospels, Jesus is the prophet.[10] And Acts, to a significant degree, is a history of the word. The "'Word of God' fills the time after Pentecost; this Word is the clamp which fastens . . . the life of Jesus and what followed."[11]

BASIC STRUCTURES

Various structure-related aspects of Luke-Acts—its overall structure, its initial structure, its opening speech, Jesus' opening speech—all reflect the Elijah-Elisha narrative.

LUKE'S OVERALL STRUCTURE

Like the Elijah-Elisha narrative, Luke-Acts consists of two balancing parts centered on an assumption into heaven. In all of ancient literature these are the only two cases of such a structure.

---

[9] Sterling, *Historiography and Self-Definition,* 363.

[10] Francois Bovon, *Luc le théologian. Vingt-cinq ans de recherches (1950–1975)* (Neuchatel/Paris: Delachaux & Niestle, 1978) 191–3; Joseph Fitzmyer, *The Gospel According to Luke (I–IX): Introduction, Translation, and Notes,* AB (Garden City, N.Y.: Doubleday, 1981) 213.

[11] Ernst Haenchen, *The Acts of the Apostles: A Commentary,* 14th ed. (Philadelphia: Westminster, 1971) 97–8.

LUKE'S INITIAL STRUCTURE

The structure of the infancy narrative (Luke 1–2) is built essentially on diptych lines,[12] a variation on the basic diptych structure found in the units of the Elijah-Elisha narrative.

THE OPENING SPEECH

In the first speech, that of the angel, the only scriptural person mentioned is Elijah: "He will go forth in the spirit and power of Elijah" (Luke 1:17).

JESUS' OPENING SPEECH

Jesus' inaugural speech at Nazareth, generally regarded as programmatic, explicitly invokes the examples of Elijah and Elisha (Luke 4:25-27). Jesus' subsequent miracles fulfil the Nazareth program, most clearly in the raising of the widow's son, when, like Elijah, "he gave him to his mother" (Luke 7:16; 1 Kgs 17:23).

SPECIFIC EPISODES

Specific Lukan passages show multifaceted affinity with specific passages from the Elijah-Elisha narrative. The shaping of the account of Stephen, for instance—the false condemnation and stoning—is modeled on the condemnation and stoning of Naboth.[13] And the raising of the widow's son (Luke 7:11-17) uses not only the obvious phrase concerning giving the child to his mother but also builds line by line on a whole section of 1 Kings 17.[14] Several other passages, including all four episodes in Luke 7, show other forms of direct literary dependence.[15]

[12] See Carroll Stuhlmueller, "The Gospel According to Luke," *JBC* 44 (1968) 24; René Laurentin, *Structure et Théologie de Luc I–II* (Paris: Gabalda, 1957) 32–3.

[13] Thomas Brodie, "The Accusing and Stoning of Naboth (1 Kgs 21:8-13) as One Component of the Stephen Text (Acts 6:9-14; 7:58a)," *CBQ* 45 (1983) 417–32.

[14] Brodie, "Towards Unravelling Luke's Use of the Old Testament."

[15] For references, see Brodie, "Intertextuality and Its Use in Tracing Q and Proto-Luke," *The Scriptures in the Gospels,* BETL 131, ed. C. M. Tuckett (Leuven: Leuven University/Peeters, 1997) 494.

CONCLUSION

The similarities of Luke-Acts to the Elijah-Elisha narrative are not secondary. Even if the striking similarities of theme are regarded as coincidence, the same cannot be said of the unique similarity of overall structure nor of the opening speeches that mention Elijah explicitly. The overall structure—two cases in all of ancient literature—is like a badge of identity. Likewise, opening speeches: they give identity. The series of specific episodes, all particularly dependent on the Elijah-Elisha text, clinch the connection.[16]

---

[16] The specific episodes also raise a problem. When taken in conjunction with some other episodes which are likewise particularly dependent on the LXX they form a distinctive stream of passages which run intermittently through Luke's Gospel and continuously through Acts 1:1–15:35, thus matching quite closely the texts sometimes attributed to the hypothetical Proto-Luke (compare Lloyd Gaston, *No Stone On Another: Studies in the Significance of the Fall of Jerusalem in the Synoptic Gospels* [Leiden: Brill, 1970] 255–6, and Brodie, "Intertextuality," 473). This is a complication, it gives fresh life to the idea of Proto-Luke, but in the long term it may also bring a basic clarification: what is based most directly on the Elijah-Elisha narrative is not the whole fifty-two chapters of Luke-Acts but a shorter version which, along with Acts 1:1–15:35, comprised the following four blocks:
- annunciations/births (Luke 1–2);
- ministry: preaching/action (Luke 3:1–4:22a [except 3:7-9; 4:1-13]; 7:1–8:3);
- death-related journey (Luke 9:51–10:20; 16:1-9, 19-31; 17:11–18:8; 19:1-10);
- death/resurrection: (Luke 22–24 [except 22:31-65]).

Acts 1:1–15:35 also consists of four expanding blocks:
- spirit promised/given (1:1–2:42);
- ministry: community, Peter's action, Solomon's porch, Sanhedrin (2:43–5:42);
- Stephen dies/ Paul reborn (6:1–9:30);
- breakthrough: Peter/Paul (9:31–15:35).

As in the case of the Elijah-Elisha narrative, each of these eight Lukan blocks consists of a diptych. For some details, see Brodie, "The Unity of Proto-Luke," *The Unity of Luke-Acts,* BETL 142, ed. Joseph Verheyden, 627–38 (Leuven: Leuven University/Peeters, 1999). This means that, quite

ELIJAH-ELISHA AND MARK

Mark's background is complex, involving influences not only from both the Greco-Roman world and the Judeo-Christian world, but also, within this Judeo-Christian world, from diverse areas. It is striking, for instance, that Mark's opening (Mark 1:1-2) coincides in part with verse one of the Primary History (*archē,* Gen 1:1), with verse one of the Pauline corpus (*euaggeliou . . . Iēsou Christou,* Rom 1:1), and with the first and last books of the prophetic corpus, Isaiah and Malachi (specifically Isaiah 40 ["A voice cries . . ."] and Malachi 3 about sending a messenger ["Behold, I send my messenger . . ."]). Without engaging the question of whether these similarities are deliberate or coincidental, they serve at some level as indications of Mark's comprehensive complexity. These similarities also help, in miniscule form, to set the scene for discussing Mark's relationship to the Primary History.

Extended analysis suggests that to some degree Mark reflects virtually the whole range of the Primary History.[17] However, there are indications that, in engaging that history, Mark gives a special role to the history's interpretive synthesis, to the Elijah-Elisha narrative. It is as though the Elijah-Elisha text serves as a lens, a foundational model, through which to engage both the larger history and other sources. Mark's use of the Elijah-Elisha text is indicated by several features.

GENRE

For Mark the world and its history are not flat or still. Rather, they are simmering with the power of God's mysterious word/kingdom, a deeper spirit-filled dimension which breaks to the surface and gives a

---

apart from Luke's relationship to Mark, there are two verifiable arguments for Proto-Luke: (1) Some texts from Luke-Acts have a precise distinctive dependence on the LXX; (2) these texts constitute eight diptychs, precisely the structure of the Elijah-Elisha narrative. It is better, however, to postpone further discussion of Proto-Luke to another work.

[17] William Swartley, *Israel's Scripture Traditions and the Synoptic Gospels: Story Shaping Story* (Peabody, Mass.: Hendrickson, 1994) 48–60, 96–115, 157–70, 203–15.

new shape to things (see, for instance, the parables of the kingdom, Mark 4). Because of this powerful underlying mystery, Jesus is not simple, nor are his disciples. They reflect the complexity and vitality of God. Jesus' identity as the Christ, for instance, is not a simple matter of information, of getting the fact straight, of telling it or keeping it secret.[18] Rather, the secrecy is expressive of mystery, in a context where mystery indicates not a lack of truth but a great richness of it. And the disciples likewise are not flat. First they are enthusiastic; next, particularly as Jesus' death approaches, they are uncomprehending and unreliable; finally, after Peter's tears of repentance and Jesus' resurrection, they are directed, with a new sense of life and purpose, to Galilee (Mark 14:72; 16:7). Thus, history has an extra mystery-filled divine dimension, and this dimension shows in people's lives.

This thumbnail summary of Mark's content helps to clarify the question of genre. Mark's Gospel is usually reckoned as a form of history or biography.[19] Adela Yarbro Collins, for instance, speaks of "apocalyptic history,"[20] and Christopher Bryan emphasizes biography.[21] It seems best to accept both dimensions: Mark evokes history, not flat history ("the bare facts"), but history as reflecting a deeper dimension, something apocalyptic that bubbles up as it were from beneath the surface. But Mark is also biographical, not that Mark gives a life of Jesus, but Mark uses Jesus' life to express the larger reality of history. Thus biography is at the service of the portrayal of mystery-filled history.

These features of Mark's Gospel—mystery-filled history expressed through biography—set the scene for comparison with the Elijah-Elisha narrative.

The Elijah-Elisha narrative consists first of all of a statement about history. Functioning as an interpretive interlude within a

---

[18] Pace Wilhelm Wrede, *The Messianic Secret* (Cambridge, N.J.: J. Clarke, 1971).

[19] For discussion, see William Telford, "The Pre-Markan Tradition in Recent Research (1980–1990)," *The Four Gospels, 1992: Festschrift Frans Neirynck*, BETL 100, ed. F. Van Segbroeck et al., 2:693–723 (Leuven: Leuven University/Peeters, 1992) 94–100.

[20] Yarbro Collins, *The Beginning of the Gospel*, 27, 34.

[21] Bryan, *A Preface to Mark*, 9–64.

narrative that runs from creation to the fall of Jerusalem, it mirrors and synthesizes history in a way that emphasizes the presence not just of bare facts but of a deeper, divine dimension, God's word, a word which effects everything from creation (1 Kings 17, rain and ravens) to death (2 Kings 13, bones and new life). In other words, the Elijah-Elisha narrative is revelatory history—essentially the same genre as apocalyptic history.

But the Elijah-Elisha narrative is also biographical. Its portrayal of history is accomplished largely through describing the lives of prophets, especially of Elijah and Elisha. Yet biography, as such, never dominates; it is subject to the more basic purpose of portraying the working of the divine in history.

What is essential is that the genre of the Elijah-Elisha narrative—revelatory (prophetic) history in biographical form—provides at least a partial precedent for the genre of Mark.

OVERALL LENGTH

One feature of Mark's account is its brevity, and the question arises as to what model it used in being so economic. Obviously Mark's length is not inspired by any of antiquity's sprawling histories. Herodotus and Thucydides, for instance, may be reckoned as four hundred pages or more. Nor is Mark's length modeled on any extended biography, not, for instance, on Xenophon's account of Socrates *(Memorabilia)* or Philo's *Life of Moses*—two works of over a hundred full pages each. Other lives are closer in volume to Mark. The biographies of Plutarch (ca. 50–120 C.E.), for example, varied considerably in length: about one hundred pages for Alexander, but only about thirty for Demosthenes.

Given the diverse volume of Greco-Roman biographies, their role as models of length is not to be excluded. But, precisely because their length varied so much, and because, in principle, Mark could have chosen to write an extended account, it is striking that the size of his Gospel (sixteen chapters) is so close to the size of the Elijah-Elisha narrative (just over nineteen chapters). The similarity of length becomes even closer if parts of the Elijah-Elisha narrative—the formulaic reigns (esp. 2 Kgs 8:16-29; 13:1-13)—are regarded as padding.

LENGTH OF EPISODES:
THE SPIRALING EXPANSION OF THE NARRATIVE

Apart from the general question of Mark's overall length, there is the more specific question about the length of particular passages and about the continuity between these passages. At first sight, the shape of Mark's materials may seem odd, or at least inconsistent, since they vary greatly. Much of the gospel is episodic and, particularly at the beginning (Mark 1, esp. 1:1-20), the episodes are very brief. But gradually, most noticeably in chapters 4–5, the episodes or materials seem to connect more clearly and to expand. Eventually, once Jesus reaches Jerusalem and cleanses the Temple (ch. 11), the narrative becomes an essentially unbroken sequence.

This gradual advance toward greater narrative continuity finds a precedent in the Elijah-Elisha narrative. At first, especially when Elijah begins (1 Kings 17), the account looks very episodic, but already in chapter 18 there is a signal of greater length and continuity; and, as already noted, the Elijah-Elisha narrative eventually concludes with an essentially unbroken block of five chapters (2 Kings 9–13).

In both narratives—Elijah-Elisha and Mark—the overall progression is not linear but spiraling. The progression from very short episodes to longer ones is followed later by a partial return to episodes that are quite short (for example, 2 Kgs 2:19-22, 23-25; 4:1-7, 38-41, 42-44; Mark 6:45-52, 53-56; 7:24-30, 31-37; 8:1-10). But this contraction makes way for further, greater expansion, and eventually for the long sequence of the conclusion (2 Kings 9–13; Mark 11–16).

Thus, overall, the Elijah-Elisha narrative provides a partial model both for Mark's quantity as a whole and also for the spiraling quantity of its various episodes.

CLEAR CONNECTIONS AT KEY POINTS:
BEGINNING, MIDDLE, AND END

Much ancient writing attached particular importance to a text's beginning, middle, and end.[22] Like the pillars of a bridge, these

---

[22] Vernon Robbins, *The Tapestry of Early Christian Discourse: Rhetoric, Society and Ideology* (London/New York: Routledge, 1996) 50–3.

three points served as the key carriers for the larger momentum of the narrative.

Precisely at these three pivotal points Mark has a clear connection with the Elijah-Elisha narrative.

BEGINNING

The Malachi-based messenger in Mark 1:2 is not anonymous; Malachi effectively identifies the messenger as Elijah (Mal 3:1, 23). Furthermore, several details of Mark 1:1-20 recall Elijah: the abrupt beginning, the wilderness, the Jordan, the prophetic speaker's external appearance, the animals/ravens, the angels, and the abrupt calling to discipleship (1 Kgs 17:3, 6; 19:4-8, 19-21; 2 Kgs 1:8).[23]

MIDDLE

The dramatic center of the Elijah-Elisha narrative—heavenly fire comes down on a mountain-top (2 Kings 1) and fire carries Elijah to heaven (2 Kings 2)—is matched in Mark, at the center, by the mountain-top drama of the Transfiguration. One mountain-top scene is of heavenly fire, the other of unearthly light. The connection between the center of Mark and Elijah is not only implied; the Transfiguration and its ensuing discussion use Elijah's name five times (Mark 9:4-13).

END

While the essential content of Mark's ending is new, its abrupt and enigmatic (16:8) manner corresponds in part to the abrupt and enigmatic account of Elisha's death and burial, including the dead man's rising to life (2 Kgs 13:21). (Is it coincidence that Mark's picture of the women fleeing frightened from the tomb is partly matched by the apparent fright of the pall-bearers and by their implied flight from the tomb of Elisha?) In any case, at an earlier point in Mark the connection with Elijah or Elisha is clear:

---

[23] Some scholars claim further affinities; see esp. Dale Miller and Patricia Miller, *The Gospel of Mark as Midrash on Earlier Jewish and New Testament Literature,* Studies in the Bible and Early Christianity 21 (Lewiston/Queenston/Lampeter: Edwin Mellen, 1990) 48–9.

as Jesus is dying his "Eloi, Eloi . . ." is followed by two explicit references to Elijah (Mark 15:35-36).[24]

FURTHER CONNECTIONS, ESPECIALLY NEAR THE THREE KEY POINTS

The connections just noted, at the three key points, are but part of a larger phenomenon, part of three clusters of connections—at Mark's beginning (ch. 1), middle (chs. 6 and 8), and end (chs. 11–16).

THE BEGINNING (MARK 1)

THE CALL OF THE DISCIPLE(S) (1 KGS 19:19-21; MARK 1:16-20). Jesus' call of the first disciples is modeled partly on Elijah's call of Elisha. Mark both simplifies and doubles the older account, thus giving extra clarity and momentum. Despite these changes the continuity appears in several aspects:

- the action begins with the caller (Elijah/Jesus) and with motion toward those to be called;
- those called are working (plowing/fishing);
- the call, whether by gesture (Elijah) or word (Jesus), is brief;
- those called leave their means of livelihood (plow/nets);
- later, the means of livelihood are variously destroyed or mended: the plow is destroyed, but the nets are mended— a typical inversion of images (showing the other side of the coin);
- after further movement, there is a leave-taking of home;
- there is also a leave-taking of other workers;
- finally, those called follow the caller.

THE HEALING OF THE LEPER (2 KINGS 5; MARK 1:40-45). Jesus' healing of a leper (Mark 1:40-45) may seem familiar, swift, and easy, but, in the entire Old Testament, an account of a specific healing from leprosy is virtually without precedent (Miriam had not previously been a leper, and her healing is simply implied rather than

---

[24] See Dautzenberg, "Elija im Markusevangelium," 1088–91.

explicitly recounted, Num 12:10-15). The one major Old Testament account of such a healing is the case of Naaman—healed by Elisha (2 Kings 5). Thus within the respective testaments the two healings are unique. This unique link is strengthened by other factors: despite Mark's brevity and differences, the two accounts retain distinct similarities, including the following:

- the action begins with the leper, and with motion toward Elisha/Jesus;
- the healer should/does extend his hand;
- the leprosy is cleansed immediately;
- there is an aftermath concerning worship (a Temple, the priest).

THE MIDDLE (MARK 6 AND 8)

THE MULTIPLICATION OF THE LOAVES. One of the most distinctive features of the chapters approaching Mark's center is the repetition of accounts of the multiplication of loaves (6:30-44; 8:1-10). In some ways the multiplication accounts dominate these chapters.

While these Markan texts involve a blending of several factors and influences, their single closest Old Testament precedent consists of the multiplying of loaves by Elisha (2 Kgs 4:42-44, next to the Naaman account). The similarities are so clear, even from a straightforward reading of the Old Testament text, that there is no need to list them.

To some degree, the figure of Elijah—and the seven-fold use of his name—runs through the entire central section of Mark (6:14–9:13). Three elements stand out: (1) Herod and the opinion that John is Elijah (6:15); (2) the miracles of the loaves (6:30-44; 8:1-10); (3) the opinion that Jesus is Elijah and the five references during and after the Transfiguration (9:4-5, 12-13).

Gerhard Dautzenberg does well in highlighting the role of Elijah in this central section and in connecting it with Jesus' cry at his death, but before attempting to distinguish hypothetical tradition from hypothetical redaction (as Dautzenberg does),[25] it is better to work with what is verifiable: the narrative of 1 and 2 Kings.

---

[25] Ibid.

THE END (MARK 11–15)

THE PURGING/CLEANSING OF THE TEMPLE. As noted earlier, both the Elijah-Elisha narrative and Mark conclude with long sequences of virtually unbroken narrative (2 Kings 9–13; Mark 11–16). The similarity between these conclusions, however, is not only one of form or shape. It is also partly one of content. Most of Mark's content, of course, is hugely distinctive. But there is also significant similarity.

As never before both narratives focus on the Temple(s). Jehu's actions reach their climax in the terrible purging and destruction of the temple of Baal (2 Kgs 10:18-27), and the aftermath in Judah centers on the takeover and renewal of the Temple in Jerusalem (2 Kings 11–12). In Mark too there is a sudden huge interest in the Temple. When Jesus reaches Jerusalem the climax of his initial visit is the cleansing of the Temple (Mark 11). Then, despite positive events in the Temple (his teaching; the giving of money, Mark 12:35-40), he goes on to speak of the Temple's impending destruction (Mark 13:1-4). The Temple is also an issue at his trial (Mark 14:57-58), and the first effect of his death is the sundering of the Temple veil (Mark 15:38).

Further broad similarities include the following: anointing and conspiracy (2 Kgs 9:1-11; Mark 14:1-14); accession (cheering, cloaks on ground; 2 Kgs 9:12-13; Mark 11:7-10); an apparent wait before taking over (2 Kgs 9:14-21; Mark 11:11); challenging the authorities (2 Kgs 9:22–10:27; Mark 11:12–12:12); giving money for the Temple (2 Kgs 12:5-17; Mark 12:41-44).

Whatever the full outline and final details, the basic point is clear: Mark's long passion narrative, while using distinctive Christian sources, coincides significantly both in form and content with the long Temple-centered sequence at the end of the Elijah-Elisha narrative. The Old Testament text does not account for Mark's narrative, but it has made an inextricable contribution. The shadow of Jehu's accession to power, especially his purging of the Baalite temple, cannot be removed from Mark's account of the cleansing of the Temple. Yet the final effect in Mark is radically different. The military and political aspects of the Old Testament account—aspects which tend to dominate—have been transformed. Yet much of the essence of the older text has not been lost. From a prophetic point of view—and the entire Elijah-Elisha narrative is primarily prophetic—the original purpose of Jehu's appointment was primarily religious, and in Mark that purpose is not lost. Rather it is restored. Therefore, the effect of leaving out the blood-thirsty details of Jehu's campaign is not to destroy the prophetic text but, in a real sense, to fulfil it.

LOCATION AND GEOGRAPHIC STRUCTURE

The Gospels' geographic settings vary considerably. Luke-Acts moves into Jerusalem and then away from it—to Samaria and the ends of the earth (Acts 1:8). In John the first place name is Jerusalem (1:19) and Jesus moves up and down several times between Jerusalem and Galilee. While Luke-Acts and John are thus quite complex, Mark's essential geographic structure is relatively simple—a basic north-to-south movement: Jesus begins in Galilee and eventually (ch. 11) enters Jerusalem.

This basic structure corresponds significantly with the overall structure of the Elijah-Elisha narrative: the two great prophets work in (northern) Israel, but near the end, in the events concerning the Temple (2 Kings 11–12), the focus switches to Jerusalem.

There are complications. In Mark, Jesus is not completely limited to a simple north-south movement. He sometimes goes elsewhere, particularly at the three key points: (1) at the beginning Jesus is in the wilderness and the Jordan (1:9); (2) near the center Jesus goes to Tyre and Sidon (7:24, 31); (3) at the end Jesus goes ahead to Galilee (16:7).

In Elijah-Elisha also there are complications, and here too they occur particularly at the three key points: (1) at the beginning Elijah is east of the Jordan and in Sidon (1 Kgs 17:2-10); (2) at the center Elijah is at the Jordan (2 Kings 2); at the end Elisha apparently faces east and Damascus (2 Kgs 13:17).

The details of these complications are debatable. What is essential is that, even in the complications, there is some affinity. Overall, therefore, both in its basic north-south pattern and in its key variations, the geographic pattern of the Elijah-Elisha narrative provides an approximate precedent for Mark.

CONCLUSION

The affinities between the Elijah-Elisha narrative and Mark are multiple: genre (blending history and biography), overall length, length and shape of many episodes, the content of the three key points, and the geographic pattern. These affinities do not take away from what is distinctive in Mark, particularly from the clarity with which Mark's long conclusion focuses on the suffering and death of just one person. Thus, in the balance between history and biography, Mark gives greater weight to biography.

But even in thus shifting the emphasis from history toward biography, Mark is following the precedent already established in principle by the Elijah-Elisha narrative. As indicated earlier, one of the basic features of this interpretive synthesis (1 Kgs 16:29– 2 Kgs 13:25) is a shift from history toward biography. Mark moves in the same direction, but further.

While there is no doubt but that Mark had his own specifically Christian sources and that he incorporated a wealth of Greco-Roman features, literary and oral, there can also be little doubt but that, in shaping these sources, he drew on the Elijah-Elisha narrative—the succinct interpretive synthesis which culminates the Scriptures' greatest history. No other explanation accounts so well for the data.

ELIJAH-ELISHA AND THE GOSPELS: GENERAL CONCLUSION

The Elijah-Elisha narrative on its own does not provide a full model for the Gospels. The Gospels are much too complex and comprehensive to be explained through a single writing. Nor is the Elijah-Elisha narrative necessarily the primary model for all the Gospels. In the case of Matthew, for example, the distinctive Old Testament literary antecedent is not the account of Elijah and Elisha, but Deuteronomy with its great discourses.

Nonetheless, when one looks at the Gospels as a group, when one seeks the primary literary thread which inspired the Gospels' mode of composition, it does not seem possible—apart to some extent from Deuteronomy—to name a document which was more central than the Elijah-Elisha narrative.

The choice of the Elijah-Elisha narrative as a central model for gospel-writing was not an arbitrary decision. The Elijah-Elisha narrative itself was central; it was a synthesis of the ancient foundational narrative (Genesis-Kings). Its content provided an avenue into the heart of the Scriptures. And its method also was hugely instructive. Insofar as the Elijah-Elisha narrative had rethought the rest of Genesis-Kings, it provided a precedent for the further rethinking of the Scriptures. The basic interpretive shifts of the Elijah-Elisha narrative, moving the emphasis from external to internal and from history toward biography, prepared the way for the evangelists to bring the process to fulfilment.

The Elijah-Elisha narrative then may be seen as the prophetic backbone which provided an initial framework for shaping the Gospels. To this framework many other features were added: infancy narratives, passion narratives, eucharistic narratives, and accounts of various miracles, discourses, and traditions.

The challenge now in speaking about the evangelists' indebtedness to Elijah and Elisha is to move beyond generalities and enter more closely into the detailed use of the actual text—the complete narrative (1 Kgs 16:29–2 Kgs 13:25). There is no a priori guarantee that the evangelists used the narrative fully, but the narrative itself had used Genesis-Kings fully, distilling it from end to end. Luke-Acts, with its close structural similarities, suggests a systematic usage, a full distilling. Such systematic usage would give fresh meaning to Luke's claim (1:3) that he had gone over the whole account from the beginning.

Detailed comparative analysis of texts is slow and difficult, sometimes even rather strange. It touches a world of imagination and artistry which appears alien to the modern emphasis on simple clear truth. And it is true that some of the literary theorizing of recent decades has been numbingly abstruse. But it is impossible to use literature (the New Testament) even for the noblest purposes without first engaging the fundamental literary questions. One of the basic features of modern New Testament research is that, in the laudable quest for history and theology, there is a bypassing of the preliminary literary spadework. This is particularly true of the quest for the historical Jesus.

In discussing the history and theology of the Gospels, therefore, a first task is not only to indicate broadly the Gospels' antecedents but to look more closely at what the use of those antecedents implies, particularly the use of the central Elijah-Elisha model.

In seeking a way forward, in seeking to clarify how the evangelists used the Elijah-Elisha narrative, it seems best to stay with Luke-Acts and Mark, or at least to give these two works special attention. It is in Luke-Acts and Mark that the signs are clearest.

Working with Luke-Acts can be tantalizing. The text is long and, while it seems evident that the present Luke-Acts used Mark, it is still not clear which has the older roots—Mark or some form of Luke.[26]

Yet, regardless of the difficulty, comparing Luke-Acts and Mark with this verifiable literary antecedent is worthwhile. A key reason is simple: in looking for a literary precedent to the Gospels there is no verifiable pre-Christian text which comes as close to any gospel as the Elijah-Elisha narrative does to Luke-Acts and Mark. If progress is to be made in tracking the Gospels' literary development and in subsequently writing history this is the avenue which seems most promising. Knowing the nature of the Elijah-Elisha narrative, its role as an interpretive synthesis, facilitates the process of investigation.

---

[26] If the existence of Proto-Luke can be verified, as seems feasible (see n. 16), then the origin of Mark becomes much less mysterious: it is inspired not only by the Elijah-Elisha narrative but by Proto-Luke's reworking of the Elijah-Elisha narrative. Given the ease of communication among early Christians (see Richard Bauckham, ed., *The Gospels for All Christians: Rethinking the Gospel Audiences* [Grand Rapids, Mich./Cambridge: Eerdmans, 1998]), Mark's awareness of all major existing Christian writings is plausible.

BIBLIOGRAPHY

Alter, Robert. *The Art of Biblical Narrative.* New York: Basic Books, 1981.

_____. *Genesis: Translation and Commentary.* New York/London: W. W. Norton, 1996.

Barr, David L., and Judith L. Wentling. "The Conventions of Classical Biography and the Genre of Luke-Acts: A Preliminary Study." Paper presented at the SBL/CBA regional meeting, Duquesne University, Pittsburgh, Pa., April 1980.

Barr, James. *The Garden of Eden and the Hope of Immortality.* Minneapolis: Fortress Press, 1992.

Barredo, Miguel Alvarez. *Las narraciones sobre Elías y Eliseo en los libros de los Reyes: Formación y teología.* Publicaciones Instituto Teológico Franciscano Serie Mayor 21. Murcia, Spain: Espigas, 1997.

Bauckham, Richard, ed. *The Gospels for All Christians: Rethinking the Gospel Audiences.* Grand Rapids, Mich./Cambridge: Eerdmans, 1998.

Boismard, Marie-E. "Elie dans le Nouveau Testament." *Elie le prophète, I: Selon les Ecritures et les traditions chrétiennes,* 116–28. Etudes Carmélitanes. Bruges: Desclée de Brouwer, 1956.

Bostock, D. Gerald. "Jesus as the New Elisha." *ExpTim* 91 (1980) 39–41.

Bovon, Francois. *Luc le théologian. Vingt-cinq ans de recherches (1950–1975).* Neuchatel/Paris: Delachaux & Niestle, 1978.

Brichto, Herbert Chanan. *The Names of God.* New York/Oxford: Oxford University Press, 1998.

Brodie, Thomas L. "The Accusing and Stoning of Naboth (1 Kgs 21:8-13) as One Component of the Stephen Text (Acts 6:9-14; 7:58a)." *CBQ* 45 (1983) 417–32.

_____. "Greco-Roman Imitation of Texts as a Partial Guide to Luke's Use of Sources." *Luke-Acts: New Perspectives from the Society of Biblical Literature Seminar.* Ed. C. H. Talbert, 17–46. New York: Crossroad, 1984.

_____. "Intertextuality and Its Use in Tracing Q and Proto-Luke." *The Scriptures in the Gospels.* BETL 131. Ed. C. M. Tuckett, 469–77. Leuven: Leuven University/Peeters, 1997.

_____. "Luke the Literary Interpreter: Luke-Acts as a Systematic Rewriting and Updating of the Elijah-Elisha Narrative." Ph.D. diss., University of St. Thomas, 1981. Available in the U.S. from University Microfilms Inc. (800-521-3042).

_____. "Towards Unravelling Luke's Use of the Old Testament: Luke 7:11-17 as an Imitatio of 1 Kings 17:17-24." *New Testament Studies* 32 (1986) 247–67.

_____. "The Unity of Proto-Luke." *The Unity of Luke-Acts.* BETL 142. Ed. Joseph Verheyden, 627–38. Leuven: Leuven University/Peeters, 1999.

_____. *Genesis as Dialogue: An Orientation Commentary. Literary, Historical and Theological.* New York/Oxford: Oxford University Press, forthcoming.

Bronner, Leah. *The Stories of Elijah and Elisha as Polemics against Baal Worship.* Leiden: Brill, 1968.

Brown, Raymond E. "Jesus and Elisha." *Perspective* 12 (1971) 86–104.

Bryan, Christopher. *A Preface to Mark: Notes on the Gospel in Its Literary and Cultural Settings.* New York/Oxford: Oxford University Press, 1993.

Burkert, Walter. *The Orientalizing Revolution: Near Eastern Influence on Greek Culture in the Early Archaic Age.* Cambridge, Mass.: Harvard University Press, 1992.

Burridge, Richard A. *What Are the Gospels? A Comparison with Greco-Roman Biography.* SNTSMS 70. Cambridge: Cambridge University Press, 1992.

Carlson, R. A. "Élisée—le successeur d'Élie." *VT* 20 (1970) 385–405.

Carmichael, Calum M. "'An Eye for an Eye, and a Tooth for a Tooth': The History of Formula." *Law, Morality, and Religion: Global Perspectives.* Ed. Alan Watson, 1–29. Berkeley: University of California Press, 1996.

_____. *Law and Narrative in the Bible: The Evidence of the Deutero-nomic Laws and the Decalogue.* Ithaca, N.Y./London: Cornell University Press, 1985.

Carroll, Robert P. "The Elijah-Elisha Sagas: Some Remarks on Prophetic Succession in Ancient Israel." *VT* 19 (1969) 400–15.

Conroy, Charles. "Hiel between Ahab and Elijah-Elisha: 1 Kings 16,34 in Its Immediate Literary Context." *Bib* 77 (1996) 210–8.

Culpepper, Alan. *Anatomy of the Fourth Gospel.* Philadelphia: Fortress Press, 1983.

Dabeck, P. "Siehe, es erschienen Moses und Elias." *Bib* 23 (1942) 175–89.

Dällenbach, Lucien. *Mirrors and After. Five Essays on Literary Theory and Criticism.* New York: City University of New York, 1986.

_____. *Le récit spéculaire. Contribution a l'étude de la mise en abyme.* Paris: Seuil, 1977.

Dautzenberg, Gerhard. "Elija im Markusevangelium." *The Four Gospels, 1992: Festschrift Frans Neirynck.* BETL 100. Ed. F. Van Segbroeck et al., 1077–94. Leuven: Leuven University/Peeters, 1992.

Douglas, Mary. *In the Wilderness: The Doctrine of Defilement in the Book of Numbers.* JSOTSS 158. Sheffield: Sheffield Academic, 1993.

Dubois, J. D. "La figure d'elie dans la perspective Lucanienne." *RHPR* 53 (1973) 155–76.

Dutcher-Walls, Patricia. *Narrative Art, Political Rhetoric. The Case of Athaliah and Joash.* JSOTSS 209. Sheffield: Sheffield Academic, 1996.

Exum, J. Cheryl. "Aspects of Symmetry and Balance in the Samson Saga." *JSOT* 19 (1981) 3–29.

_____. "Literary Patterns in the Samson Saga: An Investigation of Rhetorical Style in Biblical Prose." Ph.D. diss., Columbia University, 1976.

_____. "Promise and Fulfilment: Narrative Art in Judges 13." *JBL* 99 (1980) 43–59.

Fitzmyer, Joseph A. *The Gospel According to Luke (I–IX): Introduction, Translation, and Notes.* AB. Garden City, N.Y.: Doubleday, 1981.

Fohrer, Georg. *Elia.* 2d ed. AThANT 53. Zürich: Zwingli, 1968.

Fokkelman, Jan P. *Narrative Art and Poetry in the Books of Samuel: A Full Interpretation Based on Stylistic and Structural Analyses.* 4 vols. Assen: Van Gorcum, 1981–93.

_____. *Narrative Art in Genesis: Specimens of Stylistic and Structural Analysis.* 2d ed. Sheffield: JSOT, 1991.

Freedman, David Noel. "The Structure of Psalm 119." *Pomegranates and Golden Bells: Studies in Biblical, Jewish, and Near Eastern Law, and Literature in Honor of Jacob Milgrom.* Ed. David P. Wright et al., 725–56. Winona Lake, Ind.: Eisenbrauns, 1995.

_____. "The Symmetry of the Hebrew Bible." *ST* 46 (1992) 83–108.

_____. *The Unity of the Hebrew Bible.* Ann Arbor: University of Michigan Press, 1991.

Gaston, Lloyd. *No Stone On Another: Studies in the Significance of the Fall of Jerusalem in the Synoptic Gospels.* Leiden: Brill, 1970.

Gunn, David M., ed. *Narrative and Novella in Samuel: Studies by Hugo Gressmann and Other Scholars 1906–1923.* JSOTSS 116. Sheffield: Almond, 1991.

Haenchen, Ernst. *The Acts of the Apostles: A Commentary.* Trans. Bernard Noble and Gerald Shinn. Philadelphia: Westminster Press, 1971.

Hartmann, Gerhard. *Der Aufbau des Markusevangeliums.* NTAbh 17, nos. 2–3. Münster: Aschendorff, 1936.

Hauser, Alan J., and Russel Gregory. *From Carmel to Horeb: Elijah in Crisis.* Bible and Literature 19. Sheffield: Almond, 1990.

Hengel, Martin. *Acts and the History of Earliest Christianity.* Philadelphia: Fortress Press, 1980.

Hinnebusch, Paul. *Jesus, the New Elijah.* Ann Arbor, Mich.: Servant Books, 1978.

House, Paul R. *1, 2 Kings.* New American Commentary. Nashville: Broadman & Holman, 1995.

Keys, Gillian. *The Wages of Sin: A Reappraisal of the "Succession Narrative."* JSOTSS 221. Sheffield: Academic Press, 1996.

Kim, Ji-chan. *The Structure of the Samson Cycle.* Kampen: Pharos, 1993.

Kleinig, John W. "Recent Research in Chronicles." *Currents in Research* 2 (1994) 43–76.

Koet, Bart J. *Five Studies on Interpretation of Scripture in Luke-Acts.* SNTA 14. Leuven: Leuven University/Peeters, 1989.

Lambert, W. G. *Babylonian Wisdom Literature.* Oxford: Clarendon Press, 1960.

Laurentin, René. *Structure et théologie de Luc I–II.* Paris: Gabalda, 1957.

Letellier, Robert I. *Day in Mamre Night in Sodom: Abraham and Lot in Genesis 18 and 19.* BIS 10. Leiden/New York/Köln: Brill, 1995.

Lindars, Barnabas. "Elijah, Elisha and the Gospel Miracles." *Miracles.* Ed. C.F.D. Moule, 63–79. London: Bowbray; New York: Morehouse-Barlow, 1965.

Long, Burke. "2 Kings III and Genres of Prophetic Narrative." *VT* 23 (1973) 337–48.

Long, V. Philips. *The Reign and Rejection of King Saul: A Case for Literary and Theological Coherence.* SBLDS 118. Atlanta: Scholars Press, 1989.

Miller, Dale, and Patricia Miller. *The Gospel of Mark as Midrash on Earlier Jewish and New Testament Literature.* Studies in the Bible and Early Christianity 21. Lewiston/Queenston/Lampeter: Edwin Mellen, 1990.

Miller, J. Maxwell. "The Elisha Cycle and the Accounts of the Omride Wars." *JBL* 85 (1966) 441–54.

Moore, Rick Dale. *God Saves: Lessons from the Elisha Stories.* JSOTSS 95. Sheffield: Sheffield Academic, 1990.

Muilenburg, James. "Form Criticism and Beyond." *JBL* 88 (1969) 3–18.

Nelson, Richard D. *First and Second Kings: Interpretation.* Atlanta: John Knox Press, 1987.

Newsom, Carol A. "Bakhtin, the Bible, and Dialogic Truth." *JR* 76 (1996) 290–306.

Noth, Martin. *Numbers: A Commentary.* London: SCM Press, 1968.

Overholt, Thomas W. *Cultural Anthropology and the Old Testament.* Guides to Biblical Scholarship. Minneapolis: Fortress Press, 1996.

Polzin, Robert. *David and the Deuteronomist: A Literary Study of the Deuteronomic History.* Part 3. Bloomington and Indianapolis: Indiana University Press, 1993.

_____. *Moses and the Deuteronomist: A Literary Study of the Deutero-nomic History.* Part 1. Bloomington and Indianapolis: Indiana University Press, 1980.

_____. *Samuel and the Deuteronomist: A Literary Study of the Deutero-nomic History.* Part 2. San Francisco: Harper & Row, 1989.

Provan, Iain W. *1 & 2 Kings.* OT Guides. Sheffield: Sheffield Academic, 1997.

Robbins, Vernon. *The Tapestry of Early Christian Discourse: Rhetoric, Society and Ideology.* London/New York: Routledge, 1996.

Rofé, Alexander. *The Prophetical Stories: The Narratives about the Prophets in the Hebrew Bible: Their Literary Types and History.* Jerusalem: Magnes, 1988.

Römer, Thomas, and Albert de Pury. "L'historiographie deutéronomiste (HD). Histoire de la recherche et enjeu du debat." *Israël construit son histoire. L'historiographie deutéronomiste à la lumière des recherches récentes.* Ed. Albert de Pury et al., 9–120. Geneva: Labor et Fides, 1996.

Roth, Wolfgang. *Hebrew Gospel: Cracking the Code of Mark.* Yorktown Heights, N.Y.: Meyer Stone Books, 1988.

Sarason, Richard S. "Towards a New Agendum for the Study of Rabbinic Midrashic Literature." *Studies in Aggadah, Targum and Jewish Liturgy in Memory of Joseph Heinemann.* Ed. E. Fleischer and J. J. Peuchowski, 55–73. Jerusalem: Magnes, 1981.

Schmitt, Hans-Christoph. *Elisa. Traditionsgeschichtliche Untersuchungen.* Gütersloh: Gerd Mohn, 1972.

Schweizer, Harald. *Elischa in den Kriegen. Literaturwissenschaftliche Untersuchung von 2 Kön 3; 6,8-23; 6,24–7,20.* SANT 37. München: Kösel, 1974.

Shuler, Philip L. *A Genre for the Gospels: The Biographical Character of Matthew.* Philadelphia: Fortress Press, 1982.

Smend, Rudolf. "Der biblische und der historische Elia." *Congress Volume. Edinburgh 1974,* 167–84. VTS 28. Leiden: Brill, 1975.

Sterling, Gregory E. *Historiography and Self-Definition: Josephos, Luke-Acts and Apologetic Historiography.* NTS 44. London/New York/Köln: Brill, 1992.

Stipp, Hermann-Josef. *Elischa-Propheten-Gottesmänner.* Münchener Universitätsschriften. St. Ottilien: EOS, 1987.

Stuhlmueller, Carroll. "The Gospel According to Luke." *JBC* 44 (1968).

Swartley, William M. *Israel's Scripture Traditions and the Synoptic Gospels: Story Shaping Story.* Peabody, Mass.: Hendrickson, 1994.

Sweeney, Marvin S. "Tishbite." *Harper's Bible Dictionary,* 1078. San Francisco: Harper & Row, 1985.

Talbert, Charles H. "Prophecies of Future Greatness: The Contribution of Greco-Roman Biographies to an Understanding of Luke 1:5–4:15." *The Divine Helmsman: Studies on God's Control of Human Events.* Presented to Lou H. Silberman. Ed. J. L. Crenshaw and S. Sandmel, 129–38. New York: KTAV, 1980.

_____. *What Is a Gospel? The Genre of the Canonical Gospels.* Philadelphia: Fortress Press, 1977.

Telford, William R. "The Pre-Markan Tradition in Recent Research (1980–1990)." *The Four Gospels, 1992: Festschrift Frans Neirynck.* BETL 100. Ed. F. Van Segbroeck et al., 2:693–723. Leuven: Leuven University/Peeters, 1992.

Thiel, Winfried. "Deuteronomistische Redaktionsarbeit in den Elia-Erzählungen." *Congress Volume. Leuven 1989.* Ed. J. A. Emerton, 148–71. VTS 43. Leiden: Brill, 1991.

Trible, Phyllis. "Exegesis for Storytellers and Other Strangers." *JBL* 114 (1995) 3–19.

Wrede, Wilhelm. *The Messianic Secret.* Trans. J.C.G. Greig. Cambridge: J. Clarke, 1971.

Walsh, Jerome T. *1 Kings.* Berit Olam. Collegeville: The Liturgical Press, 1996.

_____. "The Elijah Cycle: A Synchronic Approach." Ph.D. diss. University of Michigan, 1982.

Webb, Barry G. *The Book of Judges: An Integrated Reading.* JSOTSS 46. Sheffield: JSOT, 1987.

White, Marsha C. *The Elijah Legends and Jehu's Coup.* Brown Judaic Studies 311. Atlanta: Scholars Press, 1997.

Wiener, Aharon. *The Prophet Elijah in the Development of Judaism: A Depth Psychological Study.* Littman Library of Jewish Civilization. London/Henley/Boston: Routledge & Kegan Paul, 1978.

Wink, Walter. *John the Baptist in the Gospel Tradition.* SNTSMS 7. Cambridge: Cambridge University Press, 1968.

Wiseman, Donald J. *1 and 2 Kings.* Tyndale OT Commentaries. Leicester: Inter-Varsity, 1993.

Yarbro Collins, Adela. *The Beginning of the Gospel: Probings of Mark in Context.* Minneapolis: Fortress Press, 1992.

INDEX OF MODERN AUTHORS

INDEX OF SUBJECTS AND BIBLICAL NAMES

INDEX OF MAIN BIBLICAL REFERENCES